A CHRISTIAN VIEW OF WAR and PEACE

AMG Publishers
CHATTANOOGA, TENNESSEE

A look at the spiritual battle between good and evil.

A CHRISTIAN VIEW OF

WAR *and* PEACE

SPIROS ZODHIATES, TH.D.

ISBN: 0-89957-509-9

Printed in the United States of America
07 06 05 04 03 02 –D– 6 5 4 3 2 1

CONTENTS

PREFACE

War or peace? Is a Christian supposed to submit to evil, or to resist it? We have been taught that the Lord Jesus Christ came to this world to bring peace, but did He? And if so, is it the same sort of peace that our statesmen are seeking today? What is a Christian supposed to believe? What is he supposed to do?

Isaiah prophesied that the Messiah would be called "the Prince of Peace" (Is. 9:6). Our Lord Himself, in the Sermon on the Mount, said, "Blessed are the peacemakers: for they shall be called the children of God" (Matt. 5:9). And again He said, "Resist not evil: but whosoever shall smite thee on thy right cheek, turn to him the other also" (Matt. 5:39).

Yet in Matthew 10:34, Christ declares, "Think not that I am come to send peace on earth: I came not to send peace, but a sword." And in Matthew 21:12, 13, we find Him foribly casting out the money changers from the Temple.

Are these actual contradictions? Can they be reconciled? Yes, indeed. Perhaps John 14:27 will help us to understand a little better. "Peace I leave with you, my peace I give unto you," said Christ to His disciples and then added these significant words, "not as the world giveth, give I unto you." He who has Christ, who has received Him by faith as Savior and Lord, has peace. But the very moment man makes peace with God, he finds himself at war with the devil. And those who belong to the devil also declare war on the Christian, because he is now a threat to their evil designs.

Preface

Does the Bible advocate peace at any price? If, as a nation, we are called upon to decide whether we shall sacrifice principle for the sake of "absence of war" (I cannot call it "peace"), if every other honorable solution fails, what are we supposed to do? Is the use of force ever permitted to the Christian in the content of his duty as a citizen?

Because in this generation the issue of war and peace has divided men as never before, I have decided to bring out in this separate volume a reprint of that part of my study on the Beatitudes of Christ that is devoted to peacemaking, as found in Matthew 5:9 and related passages of the New Testament. This occupied more space in my book, *The Pursuit of Happiness,* than any other Beatitude.

May the peace of God fill your heart as you study His Word to determine what it teaches about this whole issue of resistance and non–resistance.

THE PEACE THAT IS BORN OF PURITY OF HEART

Blessedness, the dwelling of God within the human heart, is the natural outcome of fulfilling certain conditions. The peace of God that follows is the crowning experience of man's obedience to Him. Christ's commandments to us, as found in the Beatitudes recorded by Matthew, are humility, sorrow, meekness, hunger and thirst for Christ's righteousness, mercifulness, purity of heart, peacemaking. These qualities, though not perceived by our physical senses, are nonetheless real, for they pertain to that which is the basis of all physical reality, that unfathomable part of the self called "spirit" or "soul."

Six of these seven spiritual qualities can be set in pairs—three on each side of the central beatitude that enjoins spiritual hunger and thirst.

Humility and meekness go together. He who humbles himself in spirit will receive such an abundance of God's mercy that he cannot help but share it with others. The helpless, who have recognized their inability to save themselves and sought Christ's mercy, cannot help sharing the mercy received with others.

Sorrow goes with purity of heart. Sorrow is the outcome of recognizing our sinful estate, at which point God steps in to cleanse us and to continue cleansing us. The fire of sorrow purifies the heart and life.

Meekness goes with peacemaking. Without meekness we cannot be peacemakers. Meekness in no way implies compromise with evil, the adoption of evil for the sake of superficial tranquillity, but a demonstration of anger against evil in order to bring it into harmony with good. The meek in Christ are the only ones who enjoy the real peace of God, the smile of God's approval for their submission to all that is divine and their reproof of all that is sinful. The meek have much in common with the peacemakers. Thus, in considering the seventh beatitude, in Matthew 5:9, we must examine it in relation to its companion beatitude in verse five, "Blessed are the meek: for they shall inherit the earth." Peacemaking is inseparably linked to meekness.

In our detailed study of meekness, we saw that it has an active and a passive aspect. Actively, meekness is anger at sin, either in our own lives or the lives of others, always with an unselfish motive. After we have registered our strong objection to sin and implemented it by whatever action God shows us to be necessary, we have fulfilled the active aspect of meekness. Passive meekness is the joyful acceptance of God's will for our lives. Meekness, therefore, is characterized by war and peace—war with evil and peace with God. It is to proclaim God's demand for holiness, and to accept the price of maintaining holiness in the midst of sin.

Dean Church once sat in the audience at an evangelistic campaign. After the service, the evangelist went to different people in the audience and asked them the rather pointed question, "Have you found peace?" Coming to Dean Church, he asked the same question, to which came the blunt reply, "No, I have found war!" Which of these men was right? The answer is, they were both right.

Peacemaking, too, consists of war and peace—outward objection and inner subjection. This is basic to our understanding of the seventh beatitude. Peace is not toleration of evil and consent to sin. That would be equivalent to covering a sore instead of healing it. The very word peace speaks of war. It is the end-product of war, the prevalence of good over evil, the reign of God in man's heart and life. But the Christian must wage the right kind of war in order to bring about the right kind of peace. It should not be the kind of peace that is temporarily gained by false meekness. In the great battle of life, there are some men who remain withdrawn from the fierceness of the struggle, in a retired and sheltered part of the field. They think this proves them to be meek, but it is quite possible that it may only prove them to be cowardly; for there is a false meekness that consists in submitting to being driven because we have not the courage necessary. Edmund Burke has said, "For evil to triumph, it is only necessary for good men to do nothing." Our Christian warfare must be motivated altruistically and not selfishly; then peace will be so abundant in our own hearts and lives that it will become contagious in the lives of others.

In the spring of the year A.D. 372, a young man in great distress of mind flung himself on the ground and burst into tears. The sins of his youth weighed heavily on his soul. Overhearing a chance conversation from a neighboring house, he was led to read the thirteenth chapter of Romans, and as a result was gloriously converted. In the language of Gaussen, "Jesus had conquered; and the grand career of Augustine, the holiest of the fathers, then commenced. A passage of God's Word had kindled that glorious luminary, which was to enlighten the Church for ten centuries . . . even to this present day. After thirty–one years of revolt, of combats, of falls, of misery; faith, life, eternal peace, came to this erring soul; a new day, an eternal day, came upon it."

As we look at the command to be peacemakers, we see that an understanding of the word "peace" is central to our discussion. First let us note its meaning in context. This beatitude follows immediately after that relating to the pure in heart. The order is first purity and then peace. It is the one who is pure in heart who has peace in his soul. Peace is the natural product of forgiveness of sin, of the cleansing of man's heart by the Lord Jesus Christ. Those whose hearts are not pure have no peace within themselves and certainly cannot impart it to others. It is of this peace that results from purity that our Lord is speaking in this beatitude, not peace as the world understands it. The phrase "Blessed are the peacemakers" does not primarily mean those who negotiate a truce between two conflicting factions, nations, or people, but those who, having experienced the peace of God as a result of forgiveness of sin, preach it to others and become the instruments in God's hands for leading others to experience the same peace. It is the peace that comes as a result, not of a compromise between opposites, but of the purification of the evil heart.

None of the qualities mentioned in the Beatitudes could be acquired by man without the supernatural intervention of God. They are God's gifts for man, the man who believes and is willing to receive them by faith. It is God alone who makes a man realize his complete helplessness and humbles him enough to call upon Christ to save and help him. It is He who makes a man sorry for sin. The natural man never considers sorrow a blessing. He alone motivates man to fight against sin and at the same time to resign himself to God's will in meekness. Man in his natural state does not hunger for the righteousness of God. God works in a man's life by emptying him of self, humbling him, purifying him in the flames of sorrow, and teaching him to conduct his Christian warfare in a spirit of meekness.

There is a calm the poor in spirit know,
That softens sorrow and that sweetens woe.
There is a peace that dwells within the breast,
When all without is stormy and distressed.
There is a light that gilds the darkest hour,
When dangers thicken and when tempests lower.
That calm, to faith and hope and love is given;
That peace remains when all beside is riven;
That light shines down to man direct from heaven.

As a result of all this, man longs to be filled with something other than self; he desires the righteousness of Christ. The overflow of that filling is mercy for others. But in sharing the purifying mercy we have received from God, we do not become impoverished and impure ourselves. The more mercy we share with others the more we experience and the purer we become in heart. It is the constant and abundant flowing of God's mercy through us that helps to keep us clean and pure. A person who keeps God's gifts to himself will lack purity of heart.

On a farm in New York State is a pond and a little brook. When I last saw them, it was in the rainy season, and both were full to the brim of clean, pure water. It is in the dry season that the difference in their natures are revealed. The stream, constantly on the go to water the banks all along its course, still keeps pure and sparkling, for it continues to draw from the underground springs at its source and to give freely as it goes along. The pond, neither receiving nor giving, hoards its precious moisture only to have its waters become foul and stagnant. It is the same lesson our Lord was always trying to teach His disciples: We gain by giving and lose by keeping. After sharing the mercy of God and thus maintaining and increasing our own purity, we receive the peace of God in such abundance that it overflows to all around us.

There are too many professing Christians today whose ultimate goal in life is to have enough for self. They lack the mercifulness, the shining purity of heart, and the peacemaking nature of which the Savior speaks. The enjoyment of peace and the sharing of it seem to be the pinnacle of the beatific edifice. For peace is one of the most potent and forceful things in all the world. It is infinitely alive. It is life at its highest and its best. There is a superficial view of life that leads men to associate the idea of peace with inertia and stagnation. True, a calm day, a waveless sea, gray boulders on the shore, are a parable of peace, if you understand that the hush in the air and the lull of the tide and the stillness of the rocks are the outcome of incalculable forces balanced and coordinated, an omnipotent equilibrium. All the vast powers of Nature go to the making of a perfect calm. As it is in the world we see, so is it in that unseen world where the soul draws its breath. There is nothing so strong and tense and vital as peace. It is spiritual equilibrium. It is the balance of that soul that is in perfect harmony with the laws of its life. And there is in every life the possibility of such harmony and the duty of seeking it (see Percy C.Ainsworth, *The Blessed Life,* London:Charles H. Kelly, 1915:145, 146).

So–called Christians whose goal begins and ends with self–satisfaction lack the abundant life, the overflowing life, of which the Savior spoke when He said, "I am come that they might have life, and that they might have it more abundantly" (John 10:10). The sharing of the life received from Christ, the sharing of His mercy, His purity, and His peace, is an evidence of our abundant life in Him.

Madame Guyon led such an abundant Christian life. Though persecuted and imprisoned for her beliefs and teachings, she had a deeply spiritual, quietly sanctified life in Christ. During her exile from the French society of her era, she wrote this poem that has since become a hymn:

> My Lord, how full of sweet content
> I pass my years of banishment.
> Where'er I dwell, I dwell with Thee–
> In heaven, in earth, or on the sea.
>
> I hold by nothing here below;
> Appoint my journey, and I go.
> Though pierced by scorn, oppressed by pride,
> I feel the good—feel naught beside.

Ah, then, to His embrace repair,
My soul, thou art no stranger there;
There love divine shall be thy guard,
And peace and safety thy reward.

She concluded, "God is not only in the soul itself, constituting its true life, but is in everything else. My soul is in such a state that God permits me to say there is no dissatisfied clamor in it, no corroding sorrow, no distracting uncertainty, no pleasure of earth, and no pain which faith does not convert into pleasure; nothing but the peace of God which passes understanding, perfect peace. Nothing is of myself, but all of God."

You can lead a miserable, predominantly selfish Christian life or an abundant one. Which one is yours?

MAN'S LOST PEACE

Before we can understand what the Lord Jesus Christ meant by the term "peacemakers" in the seventh beatitude (Matt. 5:9), it is necessary for us to understand the basic meaning of the word "peace." What is peace? We have seen in its context in the Beatitudes that it is the purity of heart that follows forgiveness of sin.

Peace in its figurative sense signifies "harmony." and figuratively is akin in thought to the Greek *homonoi,* meaning "of the same mind." The Greek word for peace is *eirēnē,* from the verb *eirō,* basically meaning "to join together." Two things, two forces, or two individuals that agree or fit together are said to be at peace with each other.

In English, the word "peace" is derived from the Latin *pax,* "an agreement," from the root verb *pac*. The basic idea is found in our common words "compact" and "pact."

What, then, is the idea of peace? Not stagnation, not stillness, not even rest. We can have rest without peace and peace without rest. Peace in Greek thought is a joining, agreement, harmony, symphony, synthesis.

Let us take an example from the physical world. Light is peace. Look at the rainbow that is the result of storm. Its colors come from the dividing up of light into its essential and constituent rays. Merge the rays and you lose the color, but you have light, and light is peace.

Take music. You hear a soprano, a contralto, a tenor, a bass—all different voices—but when they blend there is harmony, there is peace.

Observe a boat as it mightily moves on the sea. That is an illustration of peace. It is the combination in unity and activity of the elements of power. There is static power, the power restraining and holding in place, there is dynamic power, the power equal to accomplishing things; there is kinetic power, the power that lies in action. The three perfectly working together produce peace.

Not stagnation, not stillness, but harmonious realization of all the meaning and mystery of being, and the expression of that meaning and mystery in the grandeur of accomplishment—that is peace.

What is peace—human peace? In the individual life it is balance, proportion, cooperation, and consequently the doing of the things that life is made to accomplish. Balance of what? Proportion in what? Cooperation between what? Let personality be considered as consisting of spirit, soul, and body; or as consisting of intelligence, volition, and emotion. Find me a man in whom these things are balanced, and I will show you a man who is at peace. That man who is cultivating his physical powers at the cost of the mental and spiritual is never at peace. That is a disproportion of personality that means war and ruin ultimately. That man who is cultivating his spiritual activities at the expense of his physical is not at peace. Find me a man in whom these things are perfectly poised, balanced, and adjusted and I will show you a man at peace. He is not a still man, not a stagnant man, not a man at rest. He is a man at peace. Social peace is the commonwealth of gifts and service, realized and yielded. This world has never yet seen it in its perfection. We have had glimpses of it, gleams of it, occasional approaches toward it, but we have never yet seen it entirely. The world came nearest to it in apostolic times in connection with the peace in the apostolic

Church. Listen to the infinite music of the declaration: "No man said that aught that he had was his own. They had all things in common." That was peace. It was peace because those men discovered their capacities and gifts, and used them in the interests of their brethren. If a brother lacked something, then his fellow would supply it. In that commonwealth of gifts and service yielded there was peace. That is the only glimpse the world has yet had of what peace really means (see G. Campbell Morgan's sermon, "The Peace of God," in *The Christian World Pulpit,* London: James Clarke & Co., 1914, Vol 86:233–234).

When God created man, man was at peace with his Creator. This was not because God consented to fit His ideas and purposes with man's, for it was man who was created in the image of God, to fulfill His purposes. "So God created man in his own image, in the image of God created he him; male and female created he them" (Gen. 1:27). God stamped His nature, the imprint of His divinity, upon humanity. As long as man did not seek his independence from God, there was harmony, peace between the two. But Satan intervened between God and man, planting the unworthy thought that God was jealous of man, afraid that if man were to know the difference between good and evil experimentally he would become as great as God. Satan's object was to make man declare his independence of God. Because man believed Satan, he disobeyed the express commandment of God and has lived independently ever since—at war with God. The pact, the peace, was broken. Man no longer agreed with God. His desires were not God's desires. And the penalty was death. Death is the ultimate outcome of this conflict between man and God; it is the separation of man from God, which in reality is the absence of peace.

> We snap the delicate, slender threads
> Of our curious lives asunder,
> And then blame heaven for the tangled ends,
> And sit and grieve and wonder.

What does it take to restore this peace between God and man? St. Gregory of Nyssa said, "Peace is the harmony of satisfied union." God must be satisfied in His reunion with man, and man finds his satisfaction in his reconciliation with God. The union must be satisfying both to God and to man. But how can God be satisfied in this union? It was God who was sinned against and in consequence had to impose man's estrangement from Himself. It was man who caused the separation, but God who imposed it. How, then, can man blame His Creator for the warfare between them? This war was of man's making, not God's. "Sin," said St. Augustine, "is the variation of the will of the intelligent creature from the known will of the Creator." The punishment imposed by God is simply the natural consequence of His original law for man. It is only logical to grant the Creator the right to establish laws governing the tranquil maintenance of His creation. Law is a right and necessary thing, and the obedient will rejoice in it. However, we must recognize that laws are both beneficent and punitive. They provide for obedience and disobedience. Obedience spells peace between the creation and the Creator; disobedience means war. There is a sense, then, in which we may say that this war has its inception, not in man, but in God; for He who initiated peace also imposed war as the consequence of man's rejection of His peace.

In this matter of restoring man to God and thus restoring God's peace to the human heart, God again took the initiative, even as He did in creation—being the beginning, the cause of all things. He sent Christ, the eternal Second Person of the Trinity, to die and thus satisfy divine justice. "He [Christ] died for all," Paul tells us (2 Cor. 5:15). In Christ's death there is sufficient satisfaction to God for the sins of all who come to Him. God descended in Christ to bring peace to the world. But the difference between His first creation and His second is that the latter is only for those who believe, those who accept it. God took the initiative in restoring peace to the world, but since only those who desire it appropriate it, we have a world at peace and a world at war. There are only two classes of people in this world, those who are still at war with God and those who have accepted God's new offer of peace with Him through Jesus Christ, His Son. To which class do you belong? If there is war and disturbance in your soul, the fault lies with you. God has done His part. You must believe. "For God so loved the world, that he gave his only begotten Son." That's God's part in the peace making between Himself and man. "That whosoever believeth in him . . . ;" that's man's part, your part, the putting of your confidence in Christ's work. "Should not perish, but have everlasting life"; that is peace fully restored for time and eternity.

Thus we see that the peace of God is a gift to man as long as man bears the image of his Creator and obeys Him. In man's rejection of that peace, we have war, the consequence of man's sin. War is not a gift of God but a consequence imposed by God and brought about by man's sin. Christ came into this world to restore this original peace between God and man, as attested by the angels who proclaimed "Peace on earth" at His birth. "Glory to God in the highest, and peace on earth, in men of good belief" (literal translation of Luke 2:14, see Nestle's text). The word is *eudokias* in the genitive in Nestle's text (*eu,* meaning "well," and *dokeō,* meaning "think, believe") and not *eudokia* in the nominative (see Arndt and Gingrich, *A Greek-English Lexicon of the New Testament.* Chicago: University of Chicago Press, 1979:319). This indicates that the Lord Jesus came into the world, not to bring both peace and good will among men as is commonly thought, but to bring only His peace, the reconciliation between God and man, in those who will rightly believe on Him. In this verse, only peace is spoken of as coming to earth through the birth of God's Son. This peace becomes the possession of those in whom God is satisfied. His peace is for men of good belief. If you believe well—to His satisfaction, not yours—then His peace will be your portion. Christ came to restore the lost peace of God to the hearts of men who believe. Man, by believing in Christ, is once again at peace with God, his Creator.

PEACE REGAINED

When Christ died on the cross of Calvary, His death paid the penalty of sin for all who would believe. Man, in appropriating by faith what Christ did for him, regains his status before God. His peace is restored. This regaining of status before God is what Christ meant by the new birth of which He spoke to Nicodemus in the third chapter of John. In order for man once again to have the unimpaired image of God, a process of re–creation is necessary. He must be born–again. Any other expedient is mere human patchwork. The new birth restores man to God and causes God's peace to reign in man's heart once again.

This is what is troubling most people in the world today: they lack the peace of God. They look for peace everywhere except in Christ. If you want true peace, that original peace that God meant for you when He created you, you can find it only through the new birth, by believing in Christ and receiving Him as your Savior and Lord.

In Christ's teaching, whenever He referred to peace in relation to the human heart, He meant this peace of God of which He became the source for all who believe. Only as you remember this fundamental meaning of peace—the result of Christ's reconciliation of man to God—will you understand some of our Lord's paradoxical and seemingly contradictory statements.

Here is an example from Matthew 10:34–36: "Think not that I am come to send peace on earth: I came not to send peace, but a sword. For I am come to set a man at variance against his father, and the daughter against her mother, and the daughter–in–law against her mother–in–law. And a man's foes shall be they of his own household." Is this the same Christ who said in John 14:27, "Peace I leave with you, my peace I give unto you: not as the world giveth, give I unto you. Let not your heart be troubled, neither let it be afraid"? In one place He declared that He came to bring war, and in another He promised peace. How can we reconcile these statements?

We can resolve this apparent contradiction only by remembering the basic meaning of the word "peace" as harmony or reconciliation between man and God. In the first passage, Christ was speaking to His disciples, whom He had commissioned as missionaries of the Gospel. Previously He had said to them, "Behold, I send you forth as sheep in the midst of wolves: be ye therefore wise as serpents, and harmless as doves. But beware of men: for they will deliver you up to the councils, and they will scourge you in their synagogues; and ye shall be brought before governors and kings for my sake, for a testimony against them and the Gentiles . . . And the brother shall deliver up the brother to death, and the father the child: and the children shall rise up against their parents, and cause them to be put to death. And ye shall be hated of all men for my name's sake: but he that endureth to the end shall be saved" (Matt. 10:16–18, 21, 22).

There is no doubt that Christ here assumes the responsibility for this war against His disciples. While they were sinners and therefore did not rebuke the world's sin and apostasy, they were regarded as its true friends. No one will object to you as long as you agree with him. But try to interfere with people and their enjoyment of sin and you will see what happens. The war that the world (whether they be strangers or your nearest and dearest) declares against the disciples of Christ, especially when they testify of Him, is the result of the peace of God that has come to these disciples as a result of trusting Christ.

Gregory Nazianzen said, "Do they cast us out of the city? They cannot cast us out of that which is in the heavens. If they who hate us could do this, they would be doing something real against us. So long, however, as they cannot do this, they are but pelting us with drops of water or striking us with the wind."

And Leighton observes, "All the peace and favor of the world cannot calm a troubled heart; but where the peace is that Christ gives, all the trouble and disquiet of the world cannot disturb it. Outward distress, to a mind thus at peace, is but the rattling of the hail upon the roof to him that sits within the house, at a sumptuous feast."

This is the kind of peace that the early Christians possessed when faced with martyrdom, or when brought into the arena to face the lions. They came forth from their cells with a song of praise and victory upon their lips.

Generally, when men speak of peace, they do not mean the same thing that Christ means. Though words are thoughts expressed, it is necessary to examine the mind and philosophy behind the words in order to determine their real meaning. When the world speaks of peace, it means the absence of outward disturbance, no matter what the underlying cause or motive for this state of seeming tranquillity. Most of the time such peace is a forced state of acquiescence, born, not of mutual and willing agreement, but of fear of the consequences of open hostility. It is an ephemeral and shallow peace, akin to the docility on the surface of a volcano. The elements are seething inside, but the explosion is held dormant. If "peace is the harmony of satisfied union," what goes by that name in this world is merely coexistence. As long as man chooses to be independent of God, he will have to bear the resultant evils, fear and inner disturbance.

But when Christ speaks of peace, He does not refer to the acceptance of the righteous and pure man by society, but to his acceptance by God, the Author of peace. The sinful world is never satisfied with the righteous saint of God, nor is the saint of God ever able to find peace, harmony, and satisfaction in association with the world. The peace of God comes to man only when he is reconciled to God. And when he is at peace with God, he cannot help being at variance with those who are at war with God.

Paul, describing the armor of the Christian soldier, exhorted the Ephesian Christians to take unto themselves the whole armor of God so that they would "withstand in the evil day," and to stand with their "feet shod with the preparation of the gospel of peace." Even today centuries later, we still "wrestle not against flesh and blood, but against principalities, against powers, against the rulers of the darkness of this world, against spiritual wickedness in high places" (Eph. 6:12). We not only contend *for* the faith, we contend *in* our faith, and we contend *by* our faith.

> Thy hand, O Christ, is light; with sweet caressing
> It leads to peace, but only through the fray.

An incident at Valley Forge in the Revolutionary War led General Lee in later years to describe General George Washington as "First in war, first in peace, and first in the hearts of his countrymen." General Washington's Colonial regulars, ill–clad, underfed, and poorly armed, were being mercilessly slaughtered in Pennsylvania. He was so sick of war, and so disheartened by the privations of his forces and the rigorous winter, that he nearly penned his resignation to the Continental Congress who had appointed him. As he walked in the woods, he was so overcome by his grievous burden that he sank to his knees in the snow and poured out his heart to Almighty God. He pleaded for strength to continue, wisdom in directing the battle, and the championship of God on behalf of his stricken men. This was the crisis, and the tide turned for the Continental forces. God had shown George Washington that peace could not come without his execution of the present struggle, but that his heart could be at peace, even in the midst of war.

THE THREE KINDS OF PEACE

The seventh beatitude, "Blessed are the peacemakers; for they shall be called the children of God," is like the fifth, "Blessed are the merciful: for they shall obtain mercy," in that both speak of sharing God's blessings with others. In Matthew 5:9 it is peace that is shared and in verse seven it is mercy. This is not our own peace and mercy but the mercy and peace that we have obtained first from God through Christ.

Let us not forget the basic word "blessed" (*makarioi*), and the basic phrase "for my sake" (Matt. 5:11) in our study of the Beatitudes. We are blessed because of Christ. He brought God to us. War may be raging around us, but this does not affect the peace of God within. In fact, it becomes more pronounced and blessed in times of outward disturbance. The peace of God is not dependent upon our circumstances but is an inner peace of the soul.

A naval officer whose ship was being buffeted by a storm was confronted by his wife, who cried out with alarm, "Oh, how can you be so calm in such a storm?" He arose and drew his sword. Pointing it at his wife's breast, he said, "Aren't you afraid?" She instantly replied, "No, of course not." "Why?" asked the officer. "Because," rejoined his wife, "I know the sword is in the hand of my husband, and you love me too much to hurt me." "Then," said he, "remember, I know in whom I have believed, and that He holds the winds in His fist and the waters in the hollow of His hand."

We do not become blessed because of anything we may do to settle disputes in the realm of international or national affairs, or in the fields of sociology, politics, economics, labor, or even between friends. It is because we are already blessed in Christ that we can spread His peace to others. How could we possibly give to others what we ourselves do not possess? Because we are blessed, that is, indwelt by God, and have His peace in our hearts, we can share God and His peace with others. As we do this, our own blessedness increases. It is a great joy when our sins are forgiven, but it is surely just as great a joy to see God forgive others as we introduce God to them. Mercy and peace shared bring far greater joy than if we keep them to ourselves. When we share God's gifts to us, we never need fear that we shall be left with less. We either end up with more or find that we enjoy what is left far more. The life of Christian blessedness is a life of peace, not only for ourselves but for others. Our only care should be to remember that what we have to share was initially given to us by Christ. It is His peace, His mercy that we share.

As in all the other Beatitudes, the class of persons on whom the Lord pronounces His blessing (in this case, "peacemakers," *eirēnopoioi*) is preceded by the definite article *hoi,* which is restrictive. It emphasizes that this is a particular class of peacemakers, those whose peace has come to them for Christ's sake and who share it for His sake. The article here emphasizes that this is a particular class of individuals who are peacemakers, distinguishing them from all other would–be peacemakers who ultimately and in reality are not lasting peacemakers. Our Lord distinguishes Christians, who are the real peacemakers, from non–Christians, who are not really peacemakers, even though they might try to be (see A. T. Robertson's *A Grammar of the Greek New Testament,* Grand Rapids:Baker, 1977:757). This is really the benediction Christ pronounces upon His missionaries whose purpose in life is to share the peace of God with others.

If you have never experienced this joy, it may be because you are hoarding Christ's blessings instead of sharing them.

When John Broadus was sixteen he accepted Christ as his Savior and at once began to introduce others to his newfound Friend. His first convert was a school friend. These two lived most of their lives in the same city, Broadus a professor in the university, the other a truck–driver; and Broadus said that he never met the man during all those years but he touched his cap as they passed and said, "Thank you, John, thank you." "I know just what he will say when I meet him coming down the golden street of heaven," said Broadus. "It will be just what he said this morning, 'Thank you, John thank you.' "

> 'Tis worth living for this,
> To administer bliss
> And salvation in Jesus' name.

We must be careful not to limit the "peacemaking" of which Christ speaks to the settling of wars and disputes. It refers primarily to sharing God's inner peace with others through proclaiming the Gospel.

That this beatitude deals with a particular, restricted class of peacemakers, whose peace is God-given and unique, is confirmed by what the Lord Jesus said to His disciples in John 14:27, "Peace I leave with you, my peace I give unto you. Let not your heart be troubled neither let it be afraid." His peace is a gift. It is far different from the material, worldly concept of peace.

What is the significance of the Eastern salutation *shalom,* or *salaam,* meaning "Peace"? The very existence and frequency of such a salutation is a confession of the turbulence of the human heart and of the world in which we live. We talk about peace in times of war or when rumors of war threaten our security. Christ came into a world of intense turmoil. His Spirit has been at work for 1900 years. Yet there are far more wars today than ever before, and they are far more destructive. Men live in fear of imminent total catastrophe or news about the increased destructibility of atom warfare.

In a recent magazine symposium, young people were asked to write on what troubled them most in their growing years. A large percentage answered, "The threat of the atom bomb." In a world where school children must crouch against walls or beside desks in air–raid drills, it is no wonder that such fears loom large in their lives and in the lives of their parents.

"Peace I leave with you," said the Lord Jesus to His disciples. It was the peace that He had already bequeathed to them by reconciling them to God. His departure from them would not mean the withdrawing of that peace. His peace is not dependent upon His physical presence with us. It is a mystical inner peace that supersedes human attainment and comprehension. Have you ever observed a final leavetaking between two people who love each other? The other day I was called to the bedside of a dying Christian. There he lay in a coma, his wife standing beside him. The only evidence of life was his labored breathing. I held the wife's hand while I prayed with her. She knew that her beloved husband, with whom she had looked forward to taking a trip in just two days to visit two little orphans whom they supported, was never going to accompany her anywhere ever again in this life. And yet she was supremely peaceful. Her peace was not one that could be stolen by the adverse circumstances of life, or even by death, the sudden death of the husband she loved so dearly. It is this kind of peace to which our Lord refers when He says, "My peace I give unto you: not as the world giveth, give I unto you." This is the peace of blessedness and not of mere happiness; it is the peace of God and not the peace of favorable circumstances. The one is permanent and rides out the inevitable storms of life; the other is temporary and sporadic, and cannot weather the gale.

What does the expression, "Not as the world giveth give I unto you," mean? "The world" means either mankind in general or the whole external and material order of things. This is what everybody was doing and is still doing in our day, seeking peace on the horizontal level. There are three kinds of peace:

> 1. Peace from around us, the peace of human friendship—that which comes from others, when they treat us as we want to be treated.
> 2. Peace from beneath us, the peace of material possessions, which comes from having a sufficiency of this world's goods.
> 3. Peace from above us, the peace of God.

Our wish for peace usually involves a desire for harmony with our environment and for material possessions. This is a tragic and non–satisfying peace. It leads to destruction. When dying, Mahmoud ordered his treasures, apparel, and other badges of luxury to be brought to his chamber. He wept like a child and said "What toils, dangers, and fatigues of body and mind the getting and keeping of these have cost me, and now I must leave them all!"

It is inconceivable that the peacemaking to which our Lord refers is the horizontal or earthly peace. It is the heavenly peace that He Himself bestows. It is peace that transcends the limits of human love and human help. How many times in life we stand helpless before some overwhelming storm. What can we do? What can we say?

A highly successful doctor and his wife had an only child, a son, whom they adored. When it came time for him to enter military service, he became an army officer. One day he was killed in a car accident. From the third floor of their apartment building, the mother saw his casket and realized that her son was dead and not merely wounded, as she had been told. In a frenzy of grief she flung herself out the window and was killed. The sorrowing father later stood between two caskets, one bearing the dead body of his son and the other of his wife. What kind of peace was missing here? Not the horizontal or earthly, for there were many friends to express their sympathy, and plenty of money to take care of the family in great comfort. But the mother could not be reconciled to life either by human or material peace. She could have withstood the shock if she had had that heavenly peace that characterizes the blessed person. Do you have that kind of peace?

SUBSTITUTES FOR PEACE

James, that apostle of the practical who could see through all sham and pretense, vividly distinguishes between earthly and heavenly wisdom. The former he calls "earthly, sensual, devilish," while of the latter he says, "But the wisdom that is from above is first pure, then peaceable" (James 3:15, 17). This is the seventh beatitude according to James. After purity of heart comes peace—both characteristics of heavenly wisdom; and wisdom itself is a figurative name of Christ, as set forth in Proverbs chapter eight.

How deep and impenetrable is the isolation in which each human soul lives! How helpless we are to share another's deepest feelings or to express all that is in our hearts to those closest to us. We wish we could see inside another's heart and soul. But God has not relinquished this prerogative. After we have experienced all the love and fellowship of others, we dwell alone on our little island in the deep, separated by "the salt, unplumbed, estranging sea," and we can do little more than hoist signals of goodwill, and how and then for a moment stretch our hands across the "echoing straits between." Longfellow felt this most keenly when he wrote:

> Ships that pass in the night, and speak
> each other in passing,
> Only a signal shown and a distant voice in
> the darkness;

So on the ocean of life we pass and speak
one another,
Only a look and a voice, then darkness
again and a silence.

Men sigh on, not knowing what the soul wants, but only that it heeds something. Our yearnings are homesickness for heaven; our sighings are for God; just as children cry themselves asleep away from home, and sob in their slumber, knowing not they sob for their parents. The soul's inarticulate moanings are the affections yearning for the Infinite, and having no one to tell them what it is that ails them.

On they go, these sobbing children, crying out against the world's injustices with a sense of personal grievance. God has not fashioned the world to suit them, so they refuse to play by His rules. They would rather feel downtrodden and abused; it suits their self-pitying natures and gives them an excuse not to have to lift themselves up to His high level but to wallow in their own excesses and those of the world around them. "Your way is a hard way," they say resentfully, not realizing that their lack of peace comes from their failure to submit themselves willingly to a higher wisdom than their own. "Our way is the natural and right way to happiness—giving free expression to our natural desires and full scope to our egos." And so we have the rebels, who in their very defiance proclaim their lack of peace.

As F. W. Robertson says, "This disordered universe is the picture of your own mind. We make a wilderness by encouraging artificial wants, by creating sensitive and selfish feelings; then we project everything stamped with the impress of our own feelings, and we gather the whole of creation into our pained being. 'The whole creation groaneth and travaileth in pain together until now.' The world you complain of as impure and wrong is not God's world, but your world; the blight, the dullness, the blank, are all your own. The light which is in you has become darkness, and therefore the light itself is dark."

Nor can outward things give real peace. The world is all for excitement. A young man hearing a sermon on interior peace said, "It's not peace we young fellows want—it's thrills." Is that how you feel? Let me tell you, there is a supernatural thrill in heavenly peace but no peace in worldly thrills. The color of heavenly peace is not a dull gray. It is brilliantly white, even in the darkest night. This is not an outside paint job, it is inlaid. Oilcloth and linoleum may both look bright and shiny, but under the stress of daily wear the cheap oilcloth soon wears out, while the inlaid linoleum gives good service for many years. The stresses of life soon show up the shoddy material of which human peace is made, but they only bring out more brilliantly the divine peace that Christ brings to our hearts.

If a physician should say to a man in a fever, "I cannot give you anything to soothe you; here is a glass of brandy for you," that would not help to allay the fever, would it? The world comes to us and says, "I cannot give you rest; but here is a sharp excitement for you, more highly spiced and titillating to your tongue than the last one, which has turned flat and stale." That is about the best it can do. And eventually man reaches the point of satiety, and everything becomes stale and profitless.

Oh, what a confession are the rush and recklessness, the fever and the fret of our century! You go about our streets and look men in the face, and you see how all manner of hungry desires and eager wishes have imprinted themselves there. And now and then—how seldom! –you come across a face out of which beams a deep and settled peace. How many of you are there that dare not be quiet because then you are most troubled? How many of you are there that dare not reflect because then you are wretched? How many of you are uncomfortable when alone, either because you are utterly vacuous, or because then you are surrounded by the ghosts of ugly thoughts that murder sleep and stuff every pillow with thorns? The world will bring you excitement; Christ, and Christ alone, will bring you rest (see Alexander Maclaren, *The Holy of Holies,* London: Hodder and Stoughton, 1905:142).

Christ could not have pronounced His benediction on the sharing of a peace that is neither real nor lasting. It was His peace, that would be admired by others watching His redeemed children, that He wanted the blessed to share with the troubled souls of men.

But pleasure is only one substitute for peace. The person of a more serious turn of mind, conscious of a vacuum within, may turn to work to fill it. The scientist, the artist, the writer, the poet—even the perfectionist housewife—may seek to find satisfaction for a restless spirit in giving themselves untiringly and devotedly to their work. Again to no avail. Perfection always eludes them; someone is always above them as they seek to scale the mountain; self-doubt insinuates its unsettling question, "Of what use is all this in the end?"

A story is told by William Gilbert of how Dante, wandering one day over the mountains of Lunigiana, eventually drew nigh to a secluded monastery. It was at a time when his mind was wracked with internal conflict and was seeking refuge from the strife. So he loudly knocked at the monastery gate. It was opened by a monk, who in a single glance at the wan, pale face, read its pathetic message of misery and woe; "What do you seek here?" said he. And with a gesture of despair, the poet replied, "Peace." Ah, it was the same old craving followed by the same old search. But neither the solitary places, nor the anchorite's cell ever brought true peace to the afflicted heart. It comes not from without but from within. We can have it in the winter of age or the spring of youth; in the lowly cottage or the stately castle; in distressing pain or in buoyant health. The secret of it is in comradeship with Christ. You can have peace in the midst of the storm, if you have Christ. He is the shelter from the tempest, the soul's haven of rest. If we have learned to value His friendship, we have mastered the secret of the "peace which passeth all understanding."

Perhaps most tragic of all the substitutes for divine peace is that of a false religion. So many voices promise peace: the cults of the East, which are having a fashionable renaissance right now; the claims of one sect or another to be the road to fulfillment and peace with the Infinite; the devotion to one cause above all others that seems to promise a better and brighter world according to its self–styled prophets; and world communism, which produces a fanatical religious fervor on the part of its deluded followers. Even lip–service to the most orthodox Christian doctrine can be a delusion and a snare, for its adherents can claim to be following the truth and yet not attaining peace of heart.

Peace is not primarily in a set of beliefs, however correct. Peace lies in no organized movement, in no program for human or world betterment. Peace lies in a Person; it is His gift to all who will come unto God by Him. Commit yourself wholly to Christ, in all humility and without reservation, to do His will, and "the peace of God, which passeth all understanding, shall keep your hearts and minds through Christ Jesus" (Phil. 4:7).

PEACE OR A SWORD?

In Scripture we have reference to two distinct stages of the gospel. In its first stage the Gospel comes as "a sword." "Think not that I am come to send peace on earth," said our Lord. "I came not to send peace, but a sword" (Matt. 10:34). Contrast this with Paul's designation of it as "the gospel of peace." In its second and final stage the Gospel brings "peace." And the end result? War brings sorrow, peace brings joy.

This process of war and peace in the human heart inaugurated by the same causative agent, Christ, is very clearly demonstrated in the Beatitudes. Evidences of warfare are given in the first half of each beatitude. They are poverty of spirit or helplessness, mourning or sorrow, meekness—which is anger at sin and submission to God's will, hunger and thirst, the need of mercy all around us, the realization of our need of cleansing, the presence of strife, persecution: all conditions that refer to war.

The second part of each beatitude gives the product of this strife—peace. And the peace of God is what we known as the Kingdom of Heaven within us, bringing comfort, the inheritance of the earth, filling with Christ's righteousness, the greater mercifulness of God, the sight of God, being called the children of God, and the reign of God within us. All these experiences speak of the peace of God within the human soul.

It is interesting to note that the word "peacemakers" in Greek is *eirēnopoioi,* a compound word derived from two Greek words: the substantive *eirēnē* meaning," peace, harmony," and the verb *poieō,* meaning "to do, to make." There is another Greek word meaning "to do, to make," the verb *prassō.* This has to do more with the means by which an object is obtained, whereas *poieō* brings out the object or end of the act itself. The peacemakers (*eirēnopoioi*), then, of whom our Lord speaks are not merely those who make an attempt at peace, but those who establish it. Their efforts lead to results. It is the end effect that Christ refers to. The means can be multiple as far as we, the instruments of God, are concerned. We may make peace in the hearts of men and women by the way we live, simply through our blessedness. There is great power in letting people see how calm the Christian can be in the midst of storm.

I know a very dear couple in Michigan whom I count as real friends in Christ. I've stayed in their home time and again when on preaching missions in their city. The wife was saved first, and the peace of God came into her life. But her husband resisted the wooing of God's Spirit. I asked him what constituted the deciding factor that finally led him to accept the Savior. Do you know what he said? "One day I came home from work and accidentally dropped my full tool box on the rug in the living room. Not a word of complaint did my wife utter. Before she was converted, she would have raised the roof. Now she was undisturbed. She patiently and smilingly picked up the spilled tools while I stood there boiling. But that was it. I saw what Christ did to her. I took Him, too. He did the same thing to me." And I know He did, because I have never found a more patient and saintly person than he. The means of peacemaking in his life was the patience of his wife.

Then again the means may be the preaching of the Gospel, through radio, the pulpit, the printed page, a personal word of testimony—or anything else. It is not the means and their uniformity or variety that are stressed here, but that, whatever the means, God can use them effectively. This is a real encouragement to all of us, some endowed with great gifts and some with small in making the peace of God known to others. Christ reassures us that it is God who gives the end result, and not the means we employ. We are mere instruments of His peace.

A hold–up man and kidnapper was sent to prison for twelve years, and there he met Jesus Christ. While he was praying, Christ seemed to say to him, "I will come and live in you, and we will serve this sentence together," and they did. Several years later he was discharged, and just before he went out he was handed a two–page letter written by another prisoner. After the salutation, it said in effect, "You know perfectly well that when I came into this jail I despised preachers, the Bible, and everything. I went to the Bible class and the preaching service because there wasn't anything else interesting to do. Then they told me you were saved, and I said, 'There's another fellow taking the Gospel road to get a parole'; but, Roy, I've been watching you for two and a half years. You did not know it, but I watched you when you were in the yard exercising, when you were working in the shop, when you played, while we were all together at meals, on the way to our cells, and all over, and now I'm a Christian, too, because I watched you. The Savior who saved you has saved me. You never made a slip." Roy said afterward, "When I got that letter and read it through, I broke out in a cold sweat. Think what it would have meant if I had slipped even once" (*Sunday School Times*).

The verb *poieō* is also used in connection with the doing of miracles (see Matt. 7:22; 13:58; Acts 19:11). And the peacemaking that we are entreated to engage in is nothing less than the performance of a miracle. The greatest miracle that can take place in a man's life is for him to be reconciled with his Creator, God. But we must never forget that it can take place only for the sake of Christ. It is He who speaks peace to the souls of men. You and I are merely channels. In our peacemaking we should have our eyes on neither our methods nor ourselves, but on Christ, and be confident that He will accomplish His work of peace in the hearts of men. Miracles belong to the realm of the supernatural. But what a privilege for us to be counted worthy of being called to be coworkers with God as His peacemakers!

Nothing is inferred in this beatitude as to what precedes the miracle of peacemaking in the heart of a sinner. We can infer from Matthew 10:34, however, that it is the sword. What happens between the time the Spirit of God begins to act in the human heart until the peace of God is firmly established there? It is the activity of the sword that precedes the establishment of peace. This is a peace by way of judgment. Jesus did not come to sing a lullaby to humanity, or to tell it that sin does not matter and that all its wickedness will eventually be forgotten. He came in the name of God and eternal truth to declare war upon all those things that prevent peace. The sword is necessary in the interests of peace.

When the gospel first comes to men, it finds them in a state of moral insensibility. "Dead in trespasses and sins" is the apostolic description of our natural condition—not only destitute of spiritual life but morally unconscious. Just as a corpse is insensible to outward stimuli, so are we, in our natural state, insensible to the things of the Spirit. The first effect of the gospel is to arouse the dormant powers of the soul. It "convinces of sin, of righteousness, and of judgment" (John 16:8). It reveals our spiritual bankruptcy and shows us that we are guilty, perishing sinners. It produces alarm, trouble, unrest. Like the flash of lightning that shows the traveler that he is on the edge of a fearful precipice, the gospel opens the eyes of the sinner to his lost and perilous condition and fills him with anguish and dread.

When the gospel was preached by Peter on the day of Pentecost, those who heard "were pricked in their heart, and said unto Peter and to the rest of the apostles, Men and brethren, what shall we do?" (Acts 2:37). They were disturbed. The gospel was a sword–thrust to their hearts.

When Paul had a revelation of Jesus as the Lord, while journeying to Damascus, we read, "And he trembling and astonished said, Lord, what wilt thou have me to do?" (Acts 9:6).

When the gospel first came to the Philippian jailer, in an agony of fear he cast himself at the feet of Paul and Silas, saying, "Sirs, what must I do to be saved?" (Acts 16:30). Truly, in such cases the words of the Saviour are verified, "Think not that I am come to send peace on earth: I came not to send peace, but a sword."

But after this comes "the gospel of peace." To the troubled penitent Christ says, "Come unto me . . . and I will give you rest. Take my yoke upon you, and learn of me; for I am meek and lowly in heart: and ye shall find rest unto your souls" (Matt. 11:28, 29). The sins of such men are forgiven; their guilt is taken away; they are "accepted in the beloved." "Therefore being justified by faith, we have peace with God through our Lord Jesus Christ" (Rom. 5:1). The believer has the assurance of God's favor; he can take up the language of the prophet and exclaim, "O Lord, I will praise thee: though thou wast angry with me, thine anger is turned away, and thou comfortedst me" (Is. 12:1). The "spirit of bondage to fear" gives place to the "Spirit of adoption, whereby we cry, Abba, Father" (Rom. 8:15). How often we have found the air on a summer's day hot, oppressive, and stagnant. Not a breath of wind stirs the leaves that hang parched or weltering in the burning rays of the sun. The very birds are silent, as though unable to breathe. Suddenly the thunder peals, and the great raindrops patter upon the ground. Then the storm bursts forth in all its fury. Flash succeeds flash with startling rapidity, the thunder rocks the very buildings in which we are sheltered, and the rain descends in a fierce deluge. At length the storm ceases, and then what a change has passed over the scene! Before, there was a peace; but it was the peace of inanimation and death, now there is a peace, but it is the peace of blessed life The air is cool and fresh, the trees assume their verdant hues, the flowers give forth their sweetest fragrance, the birds make the groves echo again with their glad melody; in a word, all nature is peaceful with a deep, exuberant vitality. And so with the gospel; it arouses men from their deadly lethargy, producing sorrow, distress, and anguish; but after this there comes a peace, even "the peace of God, which passeth all understanding" (Phil. 4:7).

PEACE BY WAY OF THE SWORD

Although Christ's coming into a man's life brings peace, it often comes by way of the sword. There are three ways in which His coming into the heart may be likened to a sword–thrust.

First, Christ opens up the depths of sin within us. Oscar Wilde was one of the most brilliant writers of comedy that the Victorian era produced. He made a tour of the United States and lectured more than one hundred times on the philosophy of the aesthetic. But morally the man was a degenerate. He could write English of silken delicacy, but he could also write the coarsest stuff. He sowed great fields of literary wild oats. He was sentenced at last to two years imprisonment for the gravest moral offenses, and during his confinement he wrote a little book called *Out of the Depths*. Let me give you the preface:

"The gods had given me everything, but I allowed myself to be lured into sensualism. I amused myself with being a flaneur, a dandy, a man of fashion. Then tired of the heights, I became a malady and a madness. There is only one thing left for me now, absolute humility. I have lain in prison for nearly two years. Out of my nature have come despair, scorn, bitterness, rage, anguish, sorrow."

The man cried out to God in penitence. Whether his penitence was sincere or not, is not clear. Judging from his behavior in prison, according to the testimony of the warden, it was.

"O wretched man that I am!" cried Paul. "Who shall deliver me from the body of this death?" (Rom. 7:24). We were tolerably contented with our characters once, but when Christ comes we are never complacent again. John reproved the church in Laodicea because of their smug self–satisfaction in one of the most scathing denunciations of Scripture: "Thou sayest, I am rich, and increased with goods, and have need of nothing, and knowest not that thou art wretched, and miserable, and poor, and blind, and naked" (Rev. 3:17). Like the sheep that look clean enough among the summer grass, but against the background of the virgin snow look foul, so you and I never know how vile we are until the background of our life is Christ. You would have thought that when Christ filled Peter's net, Peter would have been ecstatically happy; but instead of that you have Simon Peter crying, "Depart from me, O Lord, I am a sinful man." Christ came to Simon Peter with the sword; showed him himself; taught him how dark he was. And whenever the sword–stroke of an indwelling Savior cuts into the deeps of a man's heart, the wound is very likely to be sore. Yet it is as necessary as the surgeon's scalpel, which cuts to heal. "Lord, Thy most pointed plea sure take, and stab my spirit broad awake!" prayed Stevenson. Let us therefore not flee the sword, but bare our breasts to it. In the hands of Christ, the sword wounds to heal.

Secondly, Christ calls us to a lifelong warfare. The note of warfare rings through the whole New Testament. The spirit is quickened now to crave for spiritual things, and the flesh and the spirit must battle till the grave.

> When the fight begins within himself,
> A man's worth something. God stoops over his head;
> Satan looks up between his feet—both tug—
> He's left, himself, in the middle: the soul awakes
> And grows. Prolong that battle through this life!
> Never cease growing till the life to come.
>
> —Browning

"We wrestle not against flesh and blood, but against principalities and powers" and spiritual darkness (Eph. 6:12). And the evil that I would not, that I do, and the good I would, that I do not. Paul knew the peace of God that passed all understanding, yet to Paul the Savior came bearing the sword. In the same manner our peacemaking makes a warrior of the person to whom Christ brings peace. It is a war against the evil that seeks to destroy our God–given peace. As we seek to establish the peace of Christ in the hearts and lives of others, we at the same time establish a battlefield. That's the sword the Savior spoke about as preceding His peace.

Thirdly, Christ's coming brings a sword, because His regenerating peace heightens our ideals in life. Before we believed, we may have had no objection to anything that was not of the highest moral caliber within the standards we have set for ourselves. But as the ideal is heightened by the acceptance of Christ, the old peace with the low and degenerate things of life goes and the pain of the desire for the highest begins. It is in the new conception of what life may be that the sword–stroke cuts into the heart. We are no more the children of time and mortality. We are the children of eternity and immortality. Wound and pain accompany the accomplishment of the birth of an individual. Whenever the horizon widens, there is sorrow. The sword of Christ smites through the thongs that bind us. The sword of Christ cuts down the veil that shadows us.

Look at the home of Mary and Joseph at Nazareth. Jesus comes into that home. After our Lord's birth came the flight to Egypt; then Jesus in the Temple—ah, yes! The sword is going deeper now. And when the public ministry began, and He was put to scorn, rejected, crucified, I think the sword had smitten that quiet home. It might have been so peaceful and so happy, with the laughter of children and the joy of motherhood. It might have been so peaceful and so happy if God had never honored it like this. But Jesus was born there, and that made all the difference. It could never be the quiet home again. Gethsemane was coming, Calvary was coming; a sword was going to pierce through Mary's heart. He came not to send peace, but a sword, the sword of the ideal divine peace penetrating the sinfulness of humanity.

Develop love, and you develop sorrow. Deepen the heart–life, and you deepen suffering. It is by doing that, through all the centuries, that Christ has brought the sword into our homes. One Stoic philosopher of Greece said, "Dry up these fountains of feeling"; so he made a solitude and called it peace. But Christ deepened and cleansed life's well–springs here, and that very deepening has brought the sword. I think it is worth it, not only to experience it ourselves but to bring it to others by being peacemakers, the peacemakers of the seventh beatitude. A person should not live without the sensibility of a conscience that has been touched and is being worked on by God. I would not live a life of isolation from God. This is the peace of spiritual death. I'd rather be alive unto God and at peace with Him, at war with self and evil. It is better to live vividly, in spite of the pain of resisting that which seeks to abolish peace, than to have the fingertips of all the angels grope at a heart of steel.

Our duty as peacemakers is to make people alive unto God at any cost and to cause them to realize the war that the peace of God in the human heart must wage. The peace that comes from above feels, sorrows with the sorrowing, rejoices with the victorious against sin, never lives unto itself, but concerns itself with others. That's the blessing received and the blessing given through peacemaking as taught by Christ (see G. H. Morrison, *Sun-Rise,* London: Hodder and Stroughton, 1903:158–168).

Outward life is light and shadow,
Mingled wrong and struggling right,
But within the outward trouble
Shines a healing, inward light.

War and Peace

Not to us may come fulfillment,
Not below our struggles cease,
Yet the heavenly vision gives us,
Even here, our inward peace.

PEACE IN AND THROUGH SUFFERING

In this matter of peacemaking, we don't want to fool ourselves or others. We've got to have a clear idea of what peace is not—and know that inner peace Christ spoke about, which is associated with blessedness. As peacemakers, we want to bring real peace to others and not a counterfeit; we want to tell them of the peace that brings tranquillity of soul, and not just a stoical quiet.

First, peace is not immunity from pain and sorrow, nor is it freedom to pursue our own ends. It is not independence from the interference or misfortunes of neighboring nations, and safety from annoyance and attack. Peace, in brief, does not come from having our own way in life. You don't really have peace when you are free to choose the circumstances of your life. Try an experiment with a child. Give him whatever he wishes, do his every bidding. Do you think you will have a contented, peaceful child? You know better. You will have a fretful, bewildered, unhappy little tyrant.

God the Father must often look upon us as spoiled children. We want what we want, and that is not always what He has chosen for us. We rebel against Him. If He were to give us all the desires of our heart, we still would not have peace. Self–satisfaction, maybe—not of the self God wants us to be, but of sinful, fallen self.

Christ's peace has nothing to do with freedom from trial and suffering. He says so Himself, in John 16:33: "In the world ye shall have tribulation: but be of good cheer; I have overcome the world." His peace comes to us, not because of favorable circumstances but in spite of unfavorable ones. That's what blessedness means—a state of inner sufficiency regardless of our outward circumstances, good or bad. Christ not only does not promise us immunity from injustice, slander, hatred, and all other wrongs war may inflict on his fellows, He warns us to expect them. The Christian is always in a small minority. He can never have the pleasure of shouting with the largest crowd. His standards are quite different from those of the world, and our Lord's words remain true for all time: "If ye were of the world, the world would love his own: but because ye are not of the world, but I have chosen you out of the world, therefore the world hateth you" (John 15:19).

Where has the finest literature come from—the literature of peace, joy, light, hope, inspiration, triumph? Has it come from men whose lives were free from suffering, pain, and disappointment? Sometimes, perhaps, but not very often. Most of it has come from prison cells, from blind poets, from disease–racked bodies. From the pens of those who suffered issued the literature of hope, our hymns of joy, our stories of faith. From this we see who really has peace. The outward circumstances and patterns of life are not its real essence. In large measure our outward and inward life are independent of each other. True peace does not come from external situations but from something within us—our inward sense of rightness with God, our consciousness of true purpose and an undivided heart. True peace looks at life from above. It regards heaven not only as a place to go to, but also as a condition to attain. If you possess Christ's peace, you are like a man secure in the comfort of his home while the storm rages outside. The ultimate victory of human life is this triumph of the inner spirit over the outward life. Look around you and you will see that those who are the calmest, the strongest, the most peaceful are not those whose lives have been filled with ease or frivolity. They are those who have known suffering, pain, and disappointment.

Anne Steele was an incurable invalid, in constant suffering, who knew deep sorrow. But the fruit of that experience was a hymn such as this:

Father, whate'er of earthly bliss
Thy sovereign hand denies,
Accepted at Thy throne of grace
Let this petition rise.

Give me a calm, a thankful heart,
From every murmur free;
The blessing of Thy grace impart,
And let me live to Thee.

Let the sweet hope that Thou art mine
My path of life attend;
Thy Presence through my journey shine,
And crown my journey's end.

Is the peacemaker, then, in his efforts to bring Christ's peace to others, simply to ignore the unhappy circumstances of others? Not at all. There is great value in ministering to the physical and social needs of those in trouble; but we must know that relieving their wants will not of itself bring them inner peace. Each man has two lives: the outward and the inward. Man's spirit can either conquer his circumstances, or his circumstances can overwhelm his spirit. A man's spirit may either humble and degrade itself so that man becomes its slave, or it may override all obstacles in its path and thus prove man a king.

Take a good look at the Lord Jesus in the closing days of His ministry. He grows stronger and stronger the nearer He comes to the cross. And when is it that He speaks most of peace? At the close of His ministry, when the forces opposed to Him were wild with fury and the darkest hour of His life was upon Him. He gathered His little company of disciples about Him in the upper room, and after seeking to prepare their hearts for what was to come, He ended His discourse by saying, "Peace I leave with you, my peace I give unto you: not as the world giveth, give I unto you. Let not your heart be troubled, neither let it be afraid" (John 14:27). Within a week the tragedy of the cross was accomplished and was transfigured by the triumph of the resurrection; and Christ stood among them again, probably in the same upper room, and said, "Peace unto you." Through the turmoil and the temptations of the three years of His public ministry, He had proclaimed the Kingdom of God, which is righteousness, peace, and joy, in the Holy Ghost; and these were the men who had received His word. To them He uttered this final and significant saying, which, in all that it involves, is the central and last word of biblical revelation on the subject of peace.

When Christ came into the world, the Jews were expecting a Messiah who would free them from Roman domination and establish a Jewish nation. They looked at the promise of peace as a promise from God to smite their enemies and allow them to rule over them. It is evident, however, that the Lord did not mean to establish that kind of peace at all. "Peace as a Messianic blessing is that state, brought about by the grace and loving mind of God, wherein the derangement and distress of life caused by sin are removed. Hence the message of salvation is called 'the gospel of peace' (Eph. 6:15)" [source unknown]. Paul calls this peace "the peace of God, which passeth all understanding" (Phil. 4:7). God is called "the God of peace" (Phil. 4:9). And then Paul, writing to the Thessalonians, gives the full scope of the meaning of the word peace: "And the very God of peace sanctify you wholly; and I pray God your whole spirit and soul and body be preserved blameless unto the coming of our Lord Jesus Christ" (1 Thess. 5:23). Peace is not anything less than the sanctification of our entire being by God Himself. It is not something we can acquire through our own efforts. It is a gift of God. It is the power of God that brings harmony to us. This is the real meaning of the word peace.

Nor is peace found in human friendship. You remember, when Job was in trouble, how little his friends did to make his lot more bearable. All their counsel could not bring peace to his heart; not being God-inspired, it merely aggravated his difficulties. Elihu asked Job, "When he giveth quietness, who then can make trouble?" (Job 34:29). For once he hit the nail on the head. Amy Carmichael says, "Not all the 'Elihus' in the world can make trouble when God gives quietness. They can do us no harm, they cannot spoil that inner quietness which must be if God's perfect peace is to be ours. Supposing they do succeed in disturbing us; then there is one certain and swift way back into peace: one upward look—Thy pardon, Lord; Thy stillness, Lord—and that which went from us returns. We have peace from the God of peace."

Look at the Master, fresh from Gethsemane, facing the cross, with not one brave soul to stand by Him to the end. But at the same time hear that calm, majestic utterance, "I have overcome the world." He had; not by outwardly subjugating it, but by bringing His peace—which the world does not comprehend and can neither give nor take away—into the hearts of men and women who would receive Him.

MUST THE PEACEMAKER SUBMIT TO OTHERS?

To be a peacemaker is to bring the peace of God to others. It is not to secure "peace at any price." Peace is not a state of being resigned to evil, passively suffering the whims and designs of others—whether they be nations, organizations, or individuals—for the sake of avoiding conflict and gaining superficial calm. In this respect the meaning of peace is like that of meekness: it is unalterably opposed to evil. Peace is not patching up a compromise that must ultimately break in pieces. It is not crying "Peace, peace," when there is no peace, but laying the foundations of a just peace in righteousness. "And the work of righteousness shall be peace; . . ." (Is. 32:17). That is how it is made, and the effect of righteousness is quietness and assurance forever. Peace without heroism is no peace. Peace may actually necessitate war. Peacemaking is not waiting resignedly for peace to come; it is snatching it out of the lion's jaw; it is sculpturing it out of the rough, hard, intractable material.

But immediately someone will confront us with the words of Christ in Matthew 5:38–42: "Ye have heard that it hath been said, An eye for an eye, and a tooth for a tooth: but I say unto you, That ye resist not evil: but whosoever shall smite thee on thy right cheek, turn to him the other also. And if any man will sue thee at the law, and take away thy coat, let him have thy cloke also. And whosoever shall compel thee to go a mile, go with him twain. Give to him that asketh thee, and from him that would borrow of thee turn not thou away."

How are we to understand this passage? Are these Christ's directions to His peacemakers? Do they produce a sentimental and effeminate type of Christian, a shirker, with no element of the adventurous and heroic in his makeup? The answer is, no, on both counts. Let us see why.

Although Christ assigns His Church the role of peacemaking in the world, He also marks her out to be the Church militant here on earth. Now this double character—of warlikeness and peacefulness—is not only stamped upon the Church by Christ Himself in her history, but we see it in His own life. Never was there such a peacemaker, and never, on the other hand, was there such a warrior. Never was there one who spoke so sternly as a prophet, so sharply and resolutely as a judge, so keenly, so searchingly, and so provocatively as a reformer, as Christ our Lord, Christ the Warrior, whose warfare is as a consuming fire; Christ the Peacemaker, whose words are all tenderness and love.

Here is a man in a passion. He strikes me, and I stand there and say, "Strike me again." Nine times out of ten he will do it. It is decidedly naive for some preachers to say that such a man will be so touched by my non–resistance that he will blush and let me alone. Man's sinful nature does not usually respond to such incomprehensible behavior; he regards with suspicion such unwanted humility, feeling that it is intended to subdue his spirit of superiority and conquest. What would happen if we as Christians made such behavior the general rule of our life? People would regard it as an invitation to push us around unmercifully. Did the Lord really want us to encourage evil? What would we do when such situations arose in family life?

Here are my seven–year–old son and his ten–year–old sister playing in the yard. Out of a clear sky, the boy hits the girl. Is she to stand there and take it? Is she to say to him, "Go ahead and hit me again. I want to do what the Lord Jesus says, to be hit and never hit back. I want to keep peace at any price." Do you think such an attitude would be helpful to the boy? Not if you know human nature. And what part should I as a parent play in this situation? Should I tell my daughter to go on suffering uncomplainingly at the hands of her brother, that by her passivity she is obeying Christ? In so doing we would both be encouraging my son to become a little monster; it would reduce Christ's teaching to an absurdity; and Christ, the Supreme Intelligence, never taught absurdities, nor encouraged evil.

Neither do we, His followers, under the pretense of peacemaking, have the right to ask others to continue in their evil ways. What right has a Christian to ask his assailant to continue his sadistic brutalities? Why should he ask anyone to hit him again? To do so is to confront him with an additional temptation at the point where he is least able to resist it. If my daily prayer to the Lord is "Lead us not into temptation," why should I think He wants me to lead others into temptation?

Did Christ intend us to take these words literally? We must always ask ourselves what the Lord's basic intent was in His teaching, and what final result He wanted to achieve. If the literal sense of these verses is contrary to His basic teaching, then we must believe He meant them to be understood figuratively. Suppose someone were to strike you on the right cheek. Is all that the Lord requires of you to turn your left cheek and say to your attacker, "Strike me again"? Or if someone takes your coat, is all that the Lord wants of you to give him your cloak, too? As long as we think of Christ's commands in this external, literal way, we may as well ask, "What would be the good of it?" It would be nothing more than a ceremonial act, no different from the offering of the tithes of "mint and cummin." If the mint and cummin did no good, at least they did no harm; but if men are left unredeemed, unchanged by grace, would not a literal application of these precepts only encourage them in greed and violence? Does not a bully become more and more a menace to society if no one opposes him? Is it really love to your enemy always to behave as these verses suggest?

Christ's interest is in the conversion of the evildoer. His intent in giving these illustrative commands was to suggest that our willingness to suffer should have such an effect upon the one that imposes the suffering that he will cease for very shame. If this purpose is not achieved, then our submission to further buffetings and robbery does neither the offender nor ourselves any good.

Consider that our Lord says in Matthew 5:40, "And if any man will sue thee at the law, and take away thy coat, let him have thy cloke also." That is, if you are sued at law, you are to give more than is demanded. Is that part of the peacemaking command of Christ? Would it make yourself or the other party more blessed in any way? If this is taken as laying down a universal rule for society, it would mean that we are never to resort to law for any claims made against us. That would practically mean that we are not to have laws at all in so far as it implies that no one is to stand up for his legal rights. The effectiveness of law depends on men being prepared to stand up for their rights. Yet a society in which all men always insisted on their legal rights would be a disgusting society to live in, even if we were content with much less than the spirit of the Sermon on the Mount. "The finest thing about our rights," says George Macdonald, "is that, being our own, we can give them up."

Look at Abraham and Lot. How perfect was Abraham's conduct; how miserable was Lot's! Abraham, the elder, who might have exacted all, conceded all. He said, "Let there be no strife, I pray thee, between me and thee, and between my herdmen and thy herdmen; for we be brethren. Is not the whole land before thee? separate thyself, I pray thee, from me: if thou wilt take the left hand, then I will go to the right; or if thou depart to the right hand, then I will go to the left" (Gen. 13:8, 9). And Lot, with the selfishness that is the peacebreaker, in awful contrast to the love that was in Abraham the peacemaker, made his election, and saw that the plain of Sodom was well watered and abundant; and he pitched his tent there. But he learned that the peacebreaker never can be on earth the peace–enjoyer; and Abraham learned by experience what he held in principle, that a peacemaker was not only a child of God, but was honored also by being called "the father of the faithful" (John Cumming, *Benedictions, or The Blessed Life,* Cleveland, OH: John P. Jewett and Company, 1854:207, 208).

On the other hand, do we seriously think that we are loving our enemies if we do not resist the claims of legal blackmailers? I don't think we can avoid the conclusion that were we to act in that way constantly we should be making laws and rules impossible; that it is for the advantage of all, even of those who from time to time break rules, that rules should be kept. I am quite clear that we believe that we ourselves should be made to keep rules, and that, if we love our neighbors as ourselves, we should support the maintenance of rules But here in the Sermon on the Mount we are called upon to fulfill, not to destroy, the law, and to bring love to our interpretation and application of it. We are never to say, "The law is on my side and that is an end of the matter." We are to be ready, not to give up our public concern for law, but to modify our private resentments. We are to go a long way in not standing up for our rights at those times when without danger to society we are free to do so.

Always to insist upon our rights is as unchristian as never to do so. If you are one who is ever quick to insist upon your rights, here are a few you might begin with:

> . . . What are they?
> The right to labor and to pray,
> The right to watch while others sleep,
> The right o'er others' woes to weep,

The right to succor in distress,
The right while others curse to bless,
The right to love while others scorn,
The right to comfort all who mourn,
The right to shed new joy on earth,
The right to feel the soul's high worth,
The right to lead the soul to God
Along the path the Savior trod.

—Author Unknown

PEACEMAKING OR COWARDICE?

The blessing of peacemaking has given rise to tremendous misconceptions, the greatest of which is that it provides an excuse to encourage evil. The proponents of such peacemaking make an altogether erroneous application of Christ's words in Matthew 5:39, "Resist not evil." Is non–resistance to evil the duty of the Christian peacemaker?

The nature of rules depends on how men normally behave. In the Sermon on the Mount we are called upon to be better than the norm, to have a higher standard than that of the world. But this does not alter the necessity for having rules. Most men feel that keeping inside the rules set by society is enough guarantee of good conduct. What Christ sought to do in the Beatitudes and in all His teaching was to shake men out of their "fossilized" forms. We need a dramatic striking expression like this Sermon on the Mount to pull us up out of that laziness. It says to us, "Your being within your rights and the other person being wrong is by no means an end of the matter. You ought, perhaps, to give in and give in again, even more than he is now asking. You mustn't ever shelter yourself under the guarantee of the law or the ordinary moral code. It is up to you to make the law human." Applying a rule in love is one thing; making a rule or making rules impossible is quite another. It is an easier thing and a disastrous one.

Here is another commandment of our Lord's that is often erroneously applied to peacemaking: "Give to him that asketh thee, and from him that would borrow of thee turn thou not away" (Matt. 5:42). Does that mean we are to pauperize the community, awaken in them passions of greed, indolence, fawning, lying, theft? Already our national economy is overburdened with the consequences of a false welfarism. The lazy and immoral lean heavily on the fact that if they knock hard at the door of the anxious vote–getting politician they will get all they want. And the empty–headed politician feels that he is doing his Christian duty when he gives to him that asketh him. But the more he gives the more he will be asked for. All of us know that there are couples, unfortunately too many of them, who prefer to draw on the welfare treasury for their six or eight children than for the father to go to work. After all, the welfare department pays more than the father could ever hope to earn. And so it goes. Our civilization is developing a society in which those who conscientiously work will have to care for the lazy and demanding. What Christ taught as a voluntary, discreet, and discriminating sense of philanthropy is becoming a forced encouragement of the degenerate human instincts of greed and laziness.

When someone comes to your door and asks for money, what should you do? You must try to determine whether the man is where he is, in a state of beggary, because he cannot help it or because he likes it. If the first is true, it is wrong to refuse him; if the second is true, it is a crime to help him. You must consider the end result of your action, not only on yourself but also on the person who comes to you for help. If your help will only demoralize him further, you should not give it. But if it will tide him over a bad place and help him to get on his feet again, you should do all in your power to give him a hand up.

Suppose you want to start a Sunday school in a needy community and give out handbills offering a dollar to everyone who will come. No doubt you'll attract quite a number. But do you think that you will really be helping those who come, either through the money or through your teaching? Hardly. The money will spoil the teaching, for their purpose in coming was financial rather than spiritual gain. Actually, you would be a public danger and a destroyer of morals if you were to do a thing like that. You would be setting a material goal for people while trying to achieve a spiritual end. And they would stop with what they were trying to achieve, not the good purpose you had for them in the back of your mind.

If in all circumstances of life we are to "resist not evil," why do we have locks on our doors? Isn't this contrary to Christ's command, "Give to him that asketh of thee"? Leave your door open so anyone can help himself. Is every policeman engaged in a business opposed to Christ's teaching in the Sermon on the Mount? Is Christian peacemaking an invitation to housebreaking?

The ancient Greeks chose for the protectress of Athens the Goddess of Wisdom, bearing the olive branch of peace, but they set her image in the Parthenon helmeted and bearing a spear to defend the peace that she brought to earth. This is symbolic of the Greek concept of peacemaking—not the submission of good to evil for the sake of peace, but the defense of the right in wisdom. He is no peacemaker who has no iron in his blood, no hot word of indignation at fitting times on his tongue, who is not ready, when occasion calls, to be a follower of Him who could flash forth, "Woe unto you, scribes and Pharisees, hypocrites!" and who spoke with appalling concreteness of the wrong combination of work and worship—devouring widows' houses and making long prayers. But he who seeks peace at any price must ever resort to the device of sacrificing principle for expediency. He who is adept at that exchange is regarded as a safe man. Nor in any sphere is he thought safer than in the Church. Of such expediency for the sake of peacemaking our churches are alas too full today. Never mind, say the pseudo–peacemakers, about the doctrine of the infallibility of the Bible. Don't trouble new members about the necessity of believing in the virgin birth of Christ, in His vicarious death, in His bodily resurrection, in His deity. All we want is to worship God together in peace, letting every man believe whatever he wants. This is the peace of many ecumenical churches. This is why it is failing to bring peace to the souls of men. Peace apart from truth, its appropriation and propagation, is a farce. The peace of the Church of Jesus Christ can only come through union with Him who is the Truth. The spokes of this wheel called church ecumenicity must be joined to Christ. It is in Him that we meet. There may be a group or two that are truly attached to Christ and His basic doctrine but the rest hold to a union of the rim of the wheel and not to its center. The less spokes that are joined to the hub of a wheel, no matter how perfect and round its periphery, the weaker it is. The least weight will crush it.

History confirms the judgment that the person within the Church who sacrifices principle for expediency in order to promote apparent peace is one of the most dangerous men in it. When will we awake to the fact that peacemaking is not compromising with evil at the expense of righteousness? When will we turn a deaf ear to the false peacemaker who tries to enforce his average opinions, which are not opinions at all; dupe us into the acceptance of his dull, formal decisions, which are not decisions at all; and persuade us to follow his course shaped only to drift with the current, which is a course peacefully leading to the precipice of destruction?

It is not only in the Church that such a man is dangerous. Under his shelter all abuses tend to gather. The evil that corrupts the world is not fostered mainly by bad men but by ease–loving men who will never take their stand upon principle and dare the consequences. Evil prospers so abundantly only because it can count so securely on such compliance and cowardice.

There is a very interesting old story in the Book of Deuteronomy that sets forth the instructions to the priests and officers about the preparation for a battle. The officers were instructed to go around among the soldiers and speak with them, and if they found there a man who was a coward, and who was afraid the army was going to be whipped, they were to send him home lest he have a bad influence on the other soldiers and spread his cowardice through the army. Gideon also was instructed to send home all cowards before he went to battle. These two cases show us what God thinks of cowards. He not only considers such a person of no use in a fight but thinks he is dangerous to have along. A coward is like a rotten apple in a barrel; it not only is of no value but it starts the other apples to rotting all around it. Yet courage can be cultivated like anything else. Many people who are naturaly fearful have overcome their fears through Christ and have forced themselves to stand bravely for the right.

PEACEMAKING: NOT A COMPROMISE WITH EVIL

"Blessed are the peacemakers," said our Lord. Some people seem to interpret this as saying "Blessed are those who let people get away with murder." The law of liberty in the Church or in a nation is not a license to let evil have full expression along with good. In recent years, evil has even been encouraged by several decisions of the Supreme Court of the United States and by certain of its justices. The idea seems to be that if the proponents of the gospel and morality are free to preach it, so should the proponents of immorality be at liberty to foster baseness. Justice Douglas opposed banning a particular book because postal officials or "some purity league" considered it obscene. "Should a publication whose main impact is the arousal of sexual desires be banned? A goodly part of life is the arousal of sexual desires. . . . The real purpose is to make the public live up to the censor's code of morality. . . . Sex cannot be suppressed in life. Should it be attempted in literature?" (*U. S. News and World Report,* 24 Dec. 1962, no. 52:12).

There is a point where freedom becomes license to do evil. Shall good make peace with evil and have it confirmed even in our Supreme Court? How absurd our society is. Justice Douglas says that, since sex finds its expression in life, why should it not find its expression in literature? The implication is that some citizens of the United States can publish obscene literature, and we who believe in decency and morality must tolerate it for the sake of peace. This false concept of freedom and peacemaking is the "Achilles' heel" of this great nation. It will fall or stand as we privately and nationally tolerate evil for the sake of peace. We need a revolution of morality in this country and this world, even if that means bucking the decisions of our judges. It is better to obey the Supreme Judge of all humanity, God.

Furthermore, it is all right, according to Justice Douglas, to arouse immoral feelings through the printed page; it is only when a man attacks a woman on the street that it becomes a crime. If we were only consistent and punished an act of immorality when televised or printed, the same as when actually perpetrated, we would have a much lower crime rate and it would be safer to walk the streets of our cities. Christians, raise your voices, spend your strength and money in the kind of peacemaking that refuses to tolerate evil or to compromise with those who permit it officially or unofficially, the peacemaking that never sacrifices principle for expediency.

A wholly perverted idea of Christian meekness leads some people to accept things as they are as the will of God. Serious men who have no wish to make a travesty of Christianity believe that it is the Christian temper to sit down and fold one's hands while disease festers in the dark, and injustice makes use of the civil powers, and wars are stirred up from oppression or greed of gold. They have even come to think that this is what Christ meant by being a peacemaker.

"For this purpose the Son of God was manifested, that he might destroy the works of the devil" (1 John 3:8). The mission of Christ in this world was the destruction of all evil. All evil, whether it be that of error or of sin in practice, opposes itself to the mission and purpose of Christ and His Church and must be removed if that mission is to succeed. Christianity, as far as evil is concerned, is necessarily an intolerant religion. As such it provokes strife and as such we must not fear to provoke it. Christ troubled the State and rent the Church; He created a whirlwind of infinite desire and unsatisfied longing in the heart of man. Those who went out in His name turned the world upside down. And no one has ever truly learned His spirit to this day who is not a disturber of conventions and formalities and "agreements with hell to be at peace with it." "My peace," said the Master, "I give unto you." Yet it was certainly not as the world gives it, but with Gethsemane and Calvary in it, with sin crushed and love victorious, and God's will done on a hostile earth as in a favoring heaven. His followers are those who resist unto blood striving against sin: and they and they alone are the true peacemakers. The true peacemakers are those who set good where evil was, who establish peace in time of war. When Jesus said that He was come to bring war and not peace, He meant war against evil, against Satan and the world, against evil which is an offense, against Satan the murderer, against the world where strife reigns eternally. In a word, Jesus meant to wage war against war.

And yet we, in our warfare for truth, have need to remember that we are also peacemakers. Though every peacemaker is a fighter, every fighter is not a peacemaker. To be a peacemaker we must fight in peace as well as for it. If we honestly desire truth and hate error, then we must honestly recognize truth wherever we meet it. We must take heed lest with our statement of the truth we provoke and intensify, by any fault in our statement, by any error in our conception of it, the very error that we are warring against. Only when we fight with God to guide and sustain us can we fight in love, without which no fighting is peacemaking. Love must often fight, and sometimes in anger that is part of meekness, but it must never cease to be love. All its warfare is to save, not to destroy; to pardon, not to avenge; to establish mercy and not mere justice, but this mercy not at the expense of justice. Even indignation must not only be akin to pity but be ever ready to change into it; and it must be purged of violence by knowing that sin, being folly and weakness, and not merely aggressive and wrong, is to be pitied.

Even for the economic battle, we have to do more than fight self–interest with other self–interests; for peace in the world we have to do more than oppose violence with violence. No device has ever yet been discovered whereby in such battles the weakest do not go to the wall. To have any hope of success we have to put the whole matter on the level of reverence for man as man, justice as in God's sight, pity as between fellow travelers from time to eternity, compassion as from those who need compassion, responsibility for talents, wealth, opportunity, privileges, as gifts from God wherewith to serve.

This means that no one can be a true peacemaker who has not God's peace, which is just God's love, in his heart. He must be a man the current of whose life runs too deep for earthly strife to ruffle, because it springs from the perennial fountain of pardon, grace, and eternal life. If that be the source of his power, the first need of his life will be a fellowship in worship, a fellowship where he will unite with all his brethren, master and workman, friend and foe, to look up into the face of their common Father. Especially will it be a fellowship where he will see God's face in the face that was more marred by conflict with the world's sin and sorrow than any man's, and yet in which is seen, as nowhere else, the glory of God (see *The Anglican Pulpit Library,* Vol. 9:28–32.)

Moral cowardice—how it infects our pulpits and pews! How often people will declaim at home about what ought to be done; what a shame such and such a situation is; what is wrong with this, that, and the other! But when these same men and women have an opportunity to speak up where it counts, how studiously self–effacing they suddenly become, how quiet, lest someone might think they held a contrary opinion! And so wrongs go unrighted, the weak go unchampioned, the brave man must stand alone while those who were so outspoken in private hold their tongues in public. For shame! Where would the Church be today if Martin Luther had acquiesced in the evil practices of his day? When Luther said to Erasmus, "You desire to walk upon eggs without crushing them, and among glasses without breaking them," the timorous, hesitating Erasmus replied, "I will not be unfaithful to the cause of Christ, *at least so far as the age will permit me.*" Is that your philosophy? If so, how can you face yourself in the mirror?

Be strong!
We are not here to play, to dream, to drift.
We have hard work to do and loads to lift.
Shun not the struggle,—face it: 'tis God's gift.

Be strong!
Say not the days are evil. Who's to blame?
And fold the hands and acquiesce,—O shame!
Stand up, speak out, and bravely, in God's name.

Be strong!
It matters not how deep intrenched the wrong,
How hard the battle goes, the day how long;
Faint not, fight on! Tomorrow comes the song.

—Maltbie D. Babcock

PEACEMAKING AND PERSONAL RETALIATION

Christ's teaching to turn the other cheek, resist not evil, go the other mile, as found in Matthew 5:39–42, may seem absurd in our present–day civilization, but it would be normal, natural, and logical in a different order of things, when the reign and righteousness of God is pre-eminent, as it will be in the coming millennium. Twentieth-century war may be advanced in science and technology, but man is still a sinful, selfish being. In his fallen state he loves to take rather than to give, to hurt rather than to suffer, to gain rather than to relinquish his rights, to rest rather than to work, to borrow rather than to lend. We live in a state of civilization where self is the central consideration, not God and others.

That has been the situation ever since man disobeyed God and fell in the Garden of Eden. Self has been placed above God, so that man's primary interest has been to enhance man. To be independent of and equal to God was the greatest allurement Satan could place before Adam and Eve. "For God doth know that in the day ye eat thereof [of the forbidden fruits], then your eyes shall be opened, and ye shall be as gods, knowing good and evil" (Gen. 3:5). It was too good an opportunity to miss. Why should we not be equal to God? The promotion of self: you can see it ever since in every field of human endeavor. We are blinded by self, smothered by self, buried in self—God and others can take the leavings.

Could things be different under conditions where self took a back seat? Can you conceive of an order of things under which, if a man did so forget himself as to strike you, and you offered the other cheek, it would so shame him that he would repent of his aggressive temper? Or, under some circumstances, borrowing or asking may be such a delicate matter and cost a man so much to dare to ask, that if you did refuse you would indeed be committing an un-Christian act. When has real Christianity and its principles ever had a chance since the first days of the Church, when men had all things in common and shared with those in need? We have had a little Christianity here and there in churches and among small groups, but we have never had a Christian state or a Christian country. We have never had a civilization that was based upon the principles and passions and purposes of our Lord Jesus Christ. It is only when Christianity is being tasted, where Christianity is the dominating factor, that you can decide whether it is a permanent and vital thing.

"Why are we angry?" asks Epictetus, the Stoic Greek philosopher. "Is it because we value so much the things of which . . . men rob us? Do not admire your clothes, and then you will not be angry with the thieves. They are mistaken about good and evil. Ought we then to be angry with them, or to pity them?" Our resistance to evil is wrong when it arises from our having placed too high a value on self and its possessions.

God gave the Law to Moses so that self and its manifestations might be kept within bounds. If I push my own self interests without control and restraint and you do the same, what will happen? There will inevitably be a clash. Self–centeredness is the greatest peacebreaker there is. It broke the peace between man and God and it makes peace impossible between human beings.

Somebody hits you a blow. What is your instinctive reaction? To give him only one blow in return? No, when he gives you one, you feel like giving him five. Self wants to retaliate out of all proportion to the injury done to self. If one man strikes another so that he loses an eye, the injured party feels like killing him, not merely plucking out his eye in return. The Jews believed in the latter course. When our Lord spoke of this law, He was referring to the commandments given to the Hebrews in Exodus 21:24, Deuteronomy 19:21, and Leviticus 24:20. "If a man cause a blemish in his neighbor; as he hath done, so shall it be done to him; breach for breach, eye for eye, tooth for tooth: as he hath caused a blemish in a man, so shall it be done to him again." And also, "If a false witness rise up against any man to testify against him that which is wrong . . . Then ye shall do unto him, as he had thought to have done unto his brother: so shalt thou put the evil away from among you . . . And thine eye shall not pity; but life shall go for life, eye for eye, tooth for tooth, hand for hand, foot for foot." The Mosaic Law did not exact a head for a tooth, a leg for a finger, but directed that there should be a correspondence between the harm done and the penalty inflicted. This is what our courts of law endeavor to do today: first to find out whether a person is guilty and then to impose an equitable punishment.

This determination of guilt and punishment is not a matter of private initiative but of public justice. We must not take into our hands what belongs to the courts. In Old Testament times the people had a system of public justice even as we have today. Some of the proud religionists of the day of Christ, the scribes and the Pharisees, usurped this prerogative for themselves, making the law a weapon for private revenge. But the law never gave a license to retaliate to any private individual. This would result in despotism and chaos rather than law and order.

The peacemaking our Lord taught to His disciples did not entail the abolition of courts of justice or even of the law. Civilization would degenerate to anarchy if every man were his own judge and free to mete out his own brand of justice to others. There would be as many dictators as there are men. The end result would not be peacemaking but peacebreaking. "Think not," the Lord said, "that I am come to destroy the law, or the prophets: I am not come to destroy, but to fulfill" (Matt. 5:17). Our Lord wanted to forestall any misconceptions along this line, and perhaps to refute what some were already saying about Him. The Lord came to supplement the law. He was the grace added to truth and justice (John 1:14, 17). Without truth—a standard to measure by—there could be no guilt; and where there is no guilt no grace is needed. Grace, which is Christ, stands on truth and justice. And justice demands the punishment of the evil and the reward of the good.

But how are we to answer those who make the peacemaking of the seventh beatitude equivalent to Christ's command in Matthew 5:39, "Resist not evil"? First we must bear in mind that no statement should be lifted out of context. These words taken in isolation from their context would result in absurd deductions. For instance, no parent should ever scold his child. We should stop locking our house and cars. The police force should be dismissed. People who drive through red lights should be able to do so with impunity. This would be a utopia for those who put self and its interests above everybody and everything else. That is, up to the point where they found out that it just wouldn't work.

Or take the words of Christ in Luke 14:26, "If any man come to me, and hate not his father, and mother, and wife, and children, and brethren, and sisters, yea, and his own life also, he cannot be my disciple." Taken as an independent, unrelated, universal statement, it imposes an immoral requirement, unworthy of the general character and purpose of Christ. But His hearers understood what He was saying. It was an extreme statement indicating that our primary love must be for Christ, and, in any conflict of interests between earthly loves and love of Christ, we must be willing to put Him first.

He spoke of faith removing mountains, but the removal of huge masses of rock and earth would be an unrealistic object for most people's prayers. Mountains stood for obstacles; and we pray, not to demonstrate that our prayers can move them, but for the accomplishment of some good purpose in accord with God's will.

It will help us to remember that Christ and His disciples all spoke in what may be called the Oriental idiom. They spoke as the people of Eastern lands always do, with what seems to the Western mind an exaggeration of expression, but is perfectly comprehensible to the native Easterner. Sometimes this Oriental manner of exaggeration for effect made it necessary for Christ, as He saw men taking Him literally, to modify His expressions and explain His meaning. He declared that a rich man could no more enter the Kingdom of Heaven than a camel could pass through a needle's eye. But when the disciples exclaimed, "Who then can be saved?" He said that only God could make it possible, implying that a special miracle would have to take place before a rich man could be saved.

An English teacher at Beirut, Lebanon, once said that the Bible needed little explanation to her scholars; they understood its idiom far better than she. A native of the East could tell in a few words far more clearly what Christ's command, "Resist not evil," means, than Tolstoi did in a whole book devoted to the subject. I certainly find my having been born and having lived for the major part of my life in the East extremely helpful in understanding the New Testament, which, when you come right down to it, is an Oriental book.

When you read the Bible, try to put yourself in the place of the one speaking, then in the place of the ones spoken to. Imagine yourself back in that time in history, under the circumstances and customs that prevailed in that day. Then ask yourself, "What do these particular words of Scripture mean in relation to the purpose of the one speaking, considering the condition of those spoken to, and the times and circumstances?" And the final question to ask yourself is, "How does this teaching harmonize with all the rest of Scripture?" Never try to apply a verse in isolation; you must understand it in relation to its particular context and to the whole context of Scripture.

RESISTANCE OR NON–RESISTANCE—WHICH ?

"Resist not evil," said our Lord in Matthew 5:39, and many people have felt that this is connected with the seventh beatitude in verse nine, "Blessed are the peacemakers." But what is the context of the whole passage in which this admonition is found (vv. 39–42)? The Lord is contrasting the Christian life with the Old Testament Jewish ideal, as embodied in the Law of Moses, and pointing out how that ideal had degenerated in actual practice. The Jewish ideal was to impose an equitable punishment upon the evildoer, not by the injured party but by the judges or the law of justice. The consequences of lawbreaking were inexorable. Pity was not to enter into it. There was no thought of winning over the evildoer and converting him. When Christ came, He introduced a higher concept—that of peacemaking. The Lord wants the blessed Christian to act as a peacemaker in the face of evil. How does He want us to do this?

1. By standing up for truth and seeking by all means to win others to the same Christian blessedness that we ourselves enjoy.

2. When someone attacks the truth, to resist him, but in a proper spirit and with a right motive. Christianity is predominantly a religion of the motive behind the action. We are not to do good with the expectation of attracting the favor of God, but to do

God's will because of our love for God Himself and for His glory. It is not just what we do that counts in Christianity but why we do it.

3. Our non–resistance to evil must be on the same basis—because of God and for His glory. When should we not resist evil? When no principle is at stake—when by our kind and unimpassioned behavior we can win the erring one to a softer frame of mind, in which the claims of the Gospel can be presented.

When Southey was a small boy, he tells of another boy in his neighborhood by the name of Jim Dick. A number of children began tormenting him one evening, calling him names because of his racial origin. The poor little fellow was reduced to tears and slunk away. One day Southey wanted to go skating, but his skates were broken, and the only boy from whom he could borrow a pair was Jim Dick. "I went to him and asked him for them," said Southey. "'Oh, yes, Robert, you may have them and welcome,' was his answer. When I went to return them, I found Jim sitting by the fire in the kitchen reading the Bible. I told him I had returned the skates and was under great obligations to him for his kindness. He looked at me as he took his skates and, with tears in his eyes, said, 'Robert, don't ever call me names again,' and immediately left the room. The words pierced my heart; I burst into tears, and from that time resolved never again to abuse a member of a minority group."

We resist evil only so that the truth may be maintained, not that we may get even with the enemy of truth. Retaliation, or besting another in an argument, should never be the motive of our resistance against others. The Lord never retaliated against His enemies but died that He might redeem them. If His voluntary sacrifice in going to the cross were not to be of benefit to His enemies, it would be a wasted effort, a senseless tragedy. He did not die only to satisfy the justice of God, but also for the eternal welfare of others. There was no selfish motive in His death. It was actually His resistance against sin, the evil in man. His death was the only means by which man could be redeemed. His resistance to evil could have taken the form of destruction of His enemies. And one day in the consummation of the age this will happen. But during this dispensation of grace, the central purpose of God through Christ and His followers is redemption, not punishment. That redemption can take place because of Christ's sacrifice.

If we resist evil only for the sake of seeing punishment meted out and retaliating for wrongs done to us, we are not being Christlike. We are like the Pharisees of old, who were vindictive in their application of the law. That is why the Lord had to tell the men of His day not to resist evil, since their motive was to get even rather than to reclaim the sinner to righteousness.

Here is an illustration that has made this practical in the experience of some with whom I have been associated. A man had funds entrusted to him for the purpose of spreading God's Word. But instead of purchasing Bibles and New Testaments to distribute, he was appropriating the money for himself. When his embezzlement was discovered, what was the Christian who entrusted him with the money supposed to do? Forget it? This would only embolden the embezzler to try the same thing on others. The Christian had certain responsibilities in this case. They were toward God, toward the embezzler, and toward the original donors of that money. He was faced with a conflict of responsibilities. If he let the embezzler go and he continued to defraud others, the Christian would bear part of the blame. He would actually be an accomplice. Since he allowed his donors to be defrauded, he must either make good himself what had been embezzled or try to recover it from the thief. Now in all this he was never possessed with the spirit of retaliation, but while justice was satisfied, the redemption of the soul of the culprit was sought diligently and prayerfully.

Actually, the law of the Old Testament not only asked for an equitable punishment of the evildoer in Leviticus 24:20, "Breach for breach, eye for eye, tooth for tooth," but also the absence of hatred in the execution of such punishment. "Thou shalt not hate thy brother in thine heart: thou shalt in any wise rebuke thy neighbor, and not suffer sin upon him. Thou shalt not avenge, nor bear any grudge against the children of thy people, but thou shalt love thy neighbor as thyself" (Lev. 19:17, 18). The religionists of Christ's day, however, conveniently ignored this latter injunction.

But the Lord went further in asking us to seek the conversion of the evildoer. The verb "love," in the command, "Love your enemies," is *agapate* in Greek, which speaks of a love that is unselfish, a love that is attached to its object because of the latter's need. God loves us in our sin, but His love does not pursue a policy of non–resistance toward that sin; it implies pity for us. God's love for mankind is not a compromise of holiness with sin, but the pity of holiness for sin. When in His love He resists our sin and us as we persist in sin, it is because He wants to win us.

Loving our enemies does not mean that we submissively consent to their hating us, but that we consider their enmity toward us pitiful, and seek to convert it into love. This is also true of resistance to evil. When the Lord says "Resist not evil," He means that we are to love those who try to do evil to us, by earnestly yearning and working for their conversion—even if that may involve personal suffering and loss. The motive is the same whether we resist or do not resist—the conversion of the evildoer.

Mere non–resistance to evil does not result in peacemaking as the Lord Jesus taught it; it does not bring the peace of God to the heart of the evildoer. It takes more than that. The same is true of resistance against evil. Merely to be against somebody or something is not what Christ teaches; nor does He teach that it is enough not to be against people and things. The Lord does not condone either opposition or apathy toward evil. Our Christian attitude toward it should be remedial. If it is not, our motive is wrong. It is also wrong to go on sacrificing yourself, either in resistance or non–resistance to evil, if you have ample evidence that the evildoer is resolute in his persistence in evil.

This is what the Lord meant when He said, "Give not that which is holy unto the dogs, neither cast ye your pearls before swine, lest they trample them under their feet, and turn again and rend you" (Matt. 7:6). Our Lord recognized that there are some people who are no better than pigs. It would be dangerous not to resist them. We are never to be quick to place anyone in the category of "dogs" and "swine," brutish souls who will trample our sacrifices underfoot and turn and rend us, thus becoming more confirmed in their bestiality. But neither are we under obligation to expose our tenderest relations with Christ to the spiritually coarse and rejecting. "Pearls before swine" are uncalled for sacrifices, serving no good purpose, and subjecting us to useless suffering.

On the other hand, there are those to whom kindness brings compunction and consequent conversion. Thus, in our peacemaking it is necessary to practice both resistance and non–resistance, with discrimination, judging each situation on its merits, as guided by the Holy Spirit.

CHRIST, OUR EXAMPLE IN PEACEMAKING

The words of Christ may sometimes be misunderstood, but, when taken in conjunction with His actions they will be strikingly illuminated. As we try to comprehend what He meant when He said, "Blessed are the peacemakers: for they shall be called the children of God," we shall do well to examine His life and study His example of peacemaking. The Lord Jesus went a good way along the path of non–resistance, but He was far from being what Tolstoi imagined Him to be—completely opposed to setting the record straight.

The Gospels give no instance of Christ smiting when smitten, or injuring when injured. He could have struck back had He wanted to, but He did not will to do so. Herein lies His greatness, His superiority over man. We would strike back and take justice into our own hands if we could, but He would not though He could. Great power, not controlled by the divine will, is a dangerous force indeed. Fear the person who has tremendous power and a sinful, greedy, revengeful, hate–filled nature. The will of the divinely indwelt person will exert a restraining influence on his capacity to strike, but the will of the unregenerate will misdirect his power. Power that seeks to destroy before it has tried to redeem the evildoer is not Christlike. The word "perfect" in Greek is *teleioi,* which comes from *telos,* meaning "end, goal, purpose." The test of our perfection, referred to in Matthew 5:48, is whether we are reaching God's goal for every human soul, his salvation. We must try in every way we can, including personal sacrifice, to bring this about, without compromising principle or doctrine.

The Lord could have descended from the cross when challenged to do so. But He did not want the manifestation of His power to be simply in response to human challenge, but the natural outcome of His eternally appointed task. He refused to come down from the cross in defiance of man's hate and revenge, but He arose from the grave while no man was conscious of what was going on. In the same manner we should be resistant to evil in our peacemaking because of our blessedness in Christ, rather than in defiance of the evil that confronts and challenges us. It is not to be resistance for its own sake, or in retaliation for personal affronts, but because of our belief in justice and right, for the sake of Christ.

> Am I a soldier of the cross,
> A follow'r of the Lamb
> And shall I fear to own His cause,
> Or blush to speak His name?
>
> Are there no foes for me to face?
> Must I not stem the flood?
> Is this vile world a friend to grace,
> To help me on to God?
>
> Since I must fight if I would reign,
> Increase my courage, Lord.
> I'll bear the toil, endure the pain,
> Supported by Thy Word.
>
> —Isaac Watts

Christ did resist His foes, by word, by look, by gesture. And yet He permitted Himself to be sentenced, mistreated, and crucified. He could have struck them all dead in an instant, but He chose not to do so, because then there would have been no possibility of their ever appropriating His peace through His own cross and resurrection. His was a merciful mission, offering opportunity before condemnation, salvation before judgment. He deliberately set the bounds of His resistance or non–resistance as a matter of His discreet choice. This was part and parcel, not of a prescribed philosophy of non–resistance, but of His mission of fulfilling His Father's will to save and redeem mankind. One of the focal verses of the New Testament is John 3:17: "For God sent not his Son into the world to condemn the world; but that the world through him might be saved." Striking His enemies dead would certainly not be accomplishing this purpose. He had to suffer at the hands of evil men in fulfillment of His mission. This was not submitting to their evil but to God's justice, which required the payment of the penalty of sin. Had Christ fully resisted evil, it would have been tantamount to the destruction of evil men by force. But His purpose was the redemption of evil men through whatever personal sacrifice was necessary. In His first coming, Christ resisted evil only to the degree necessary to show people that He was neither the author nor the supporter of it. He did not resist beyond the point where His resistance would hinder the purpose for which He came. We see, then, that He came to resist evil and at the same time to redeem men from it. He would not allow His first purpose to hinder His second, nor the second to cancel out the first.

This is why we find Christ seemingly acquiescent toward evil on occasion. He forbade force to be employed in His defense against His cruel foes. "Put up again thy sword into his place: for all they that take the sword shall perish with the sword" (Matt. 26:52), He said to Peter, who had cut off the ear of one of the soldiers who came to arrest Him. This was useless resistance. Its end result could not have been the redemption of the Roman soldier. And Christ, in spite of constant remonstrances from His disciples, did not wish to be spared from the cross. He could have avoided it but He would not, for your sake and mine. Praise God that He didn't! He surrendered Himself and was led away. He could have summoned twelve legions of angels to rescue Him, but He would not.

Our resistance to evil must fit within the framework of God's purpose. It should not be aimless. It should lead to peacemaking, that is, reconciling men to God. Was Christ referring to Peter when He said, "They that take the sword shall perish with the sword"? It is more likely that He was referring to the armed soldiers who came to apprehend Him. "Leave them alone," said Christ. "They rely on the sword, they hate Me and reject My salvation; their final end shall be judgment—the sword" (author's paraphrase).

Observe Christ in court. His accusers were unable to find any two witnesses whose testimony against Him would agree. Finally the High Priest called Jesus to the stand and administered the oath. "I adjure thee by the living God, that thou tell us whether thou be the Christ, the Son of God" (Matt. 26:63). Jesus protested, "If I tell you, ye will not believe" (Luke 22:67). Yet He freely bore His testimony, declared that He was the Son of God, and was led away to His death.

One day Jesus wanted to travel from Galilee in the north to Jerusalem, where He would ultimately die—not because of His inability to resist and subjugate evil, but because it was His Father's will for Him to do so. As Samaria lay between Galilee and Judea, He sent messengers to Samaria, who asked the inhabitants of a certain village to make ready for Jesus' passing through. They refused to receive Him, which greatly angered His disciples. James and John returned to Jesus and said. "Lord, wilt thou that we command fire to come down from heaven, and consume them, even as Elias did?" Now, they could have done this, if Jesus had given them the powers and He had it to give them. Observe how He rebuked them: "Ye know not what manner of spirit ye are of. For the Son of man is not come to destroy men's lives, but to save them" (Luke 9:51–56).

Notice that these incidents were connected with His death at Jerusalem for the sake of reconciling man to God. He would let nothing stand in the way of the perfect consummation of His life in death—an end that would be the beginning of eternal life for you and me.

A Chinese Emperor, upon being told that his enemies had raised an insurrection in one of the distant provinces, said, "Come, then, my friends, follow me, and I promise you that we shall quickly destroy them." He marched forward, and the rebels submitted at his approach. All now thought that he would take the most signal revenge, but were surprised to see the captives treated with mildness and humanity. "How!" cried the First Minister, "is this the manner in which you fulfill your promise? Your royal word was given that your enemies should be destroyed, and behold you have pardoned them all, and even caressed some of them!" "I promised," replied the Emperor, with a generous air, "to destroy my enemies; I have fulfilled my word; for, see, they are enemies no longer: I have made friends of them."

Christ has two ways of destroying His enemies: one is to win them by love, as exemplified in His death on the cross; the other is to let them reap the consequences of their rejection of Him in the final judgment. "Greater love hath no man than this, that a man lay down his life for his friends . . . . But God commendeth his love toward us, in that, while we were yet sinners, Christ died for us" (John 15:13; Rom. 5:8). What more can He do to make peace with His enemies? Yours is the choice: Will you be won over by love through accepting His atoning work on the cross for you; or must you await the final judgment in fear and trembling?

RESISTING IN LOVE

Though Christ protested against evil on many occasions in His life, and even took action against it, His resistance to man and man's wickedness was never such as to hinder Him from being completely subject to the will of His Father. He had come into the world to save sinners, to destroy the works of the devil, and nothing must be allowed to divert Him from His mission. When you remember this, you will see where His resistance found its place in the total framework of His life. Christ resisted evil and rebuked His foes by look, by word, by gesture. Think of His words to Ruler and Pharisee and Scribe. They were awful in their severity—among the sternest ever spoken. Did He always quietly submit to the anger of His foes? No, only if that submission would further the total plan and purpose for which He came into the world.

As He is, so are we in this world, the Bible tells us. Our resistance or non–resistance to evil must have the same motivation—to win souls and overcome wickedness for Christ's sake. We not only have no right to resent and avenge personal affronts, but we also have no right to let affronts to God and others go unchecked and unchallenged. We are to have neither the "tit–for–tat" spirit nor the *laissez–faire* spirit.

On one occasion, when His countrymen sought to cast Him from the brow of the hill whereon their city stood, we read, "He passing through the midst of them went his way" (Luke 4:30). Did He always offer the other cheek when He had been smitten? He did not do so in the presence of the High Priest, but asked in remonstrance, "Why smitest thou me?" He wanted to submit, and He did, but not without a protest. We, too, should be true protestants in the presence of evil, remembering, nevertheless, that we have a God above to whom we owe submission. Never yield to evil, but to God, who may permit it to accomplish His divinely and mysteriously appointed will. We may be sure that even the most literal–minded of our Lord's hearers would not have felt bound to offer his cloak to one who had stolen his coat. He understood that our Lord meant to apply a principle here, that we are not to value our material possessions above winning over an enemy for Christ. In this connection, I like a little motto that used to hang in the lobby of Shelton College:

Hail, Guest, we ask not what thou art;
If friend, we greet thee, hand and heart;
If stranger, such no longer be,
If foe, our love shall conquer thee.

When Christ went up to the temple, a corrupt and wicked government had put cattle in the one court where the Gentiles might go. He did not merely utter a verbal protest against it; He wove a whip of small cords of the straw that was at His feet and, with flashing eye and with thunderous tones, drove the frightened traders from the temple with their cattle, and overturned the money changers' tables, leaving the money to roll about the floor.

When the temple band came to arrest Him, and His disciples were defenseless in Gethsemane, Christ went forward and put Himself between the disciples and the band, which fell backward to the ground. For the moment, He confronted them and held them at bay, that His disciples might escape, and then, and not till then, surrendered Himself. Christ used force to defend others but never to defend Himself. The fundamental principle in Christ's teaching is this: Love may use combativeness; selfishness may not. The wrath, says the Book of Revelation, is the wrath of the Lamb. There is a combativeness motivated by love that is legitimate. If the highwayman demands my purse, I may hand it over to him rather than take his life, and frankly confess, were I ever so brave, I think I would rather go without my purse than have the blood even of a guilty man on my hands. But if he assaults my wife or my children, whom God has put in my keeping, that is another matter; then, if I do not defend them, I am a coward and a criminal. Our lives are so intertwined with one another that it is often impossible to tell whether we are defending ourselves or another. It is spirit, not rule or regulation, which Christ prescribes, and this is the spirit: Love may fight; selfishness may not. To a considerable extent modern civilization accepts this principle. In a barbaric community every man carries a pistol in his hip pocket. We civilized communities do not. We trust other men to be our defenders and protectors (see Lyman Abbot's sermon, "War or Peace," in *The Christian World Pulpit,* 11 March 1986, Vol. 49: 169–172).

As we saw in our studies on meekness and in our examination of Christ as the meek and humble One, the divine method is not passive but active in relation to evil. God resists evil, not passively, watching it without involvement and hoping for the best, but by doing something for its reversal, for the establishment of righteousness in its place. There is a moral order in the world, which, if we go against, will slowly but surely bring retribution upon us.

> Though the mills of God grind slowly,
> Yet they grind exceeding small;
> Though with patience He stands waiting,
> With exactness, grinds He all.
> —Author Unknown

Surely we are in line with that order when, with pity in our hearts for the sinner, we resist his sin. This is what is involved in our peacemaking. Christ Himself looked round upon His foes "with anger, being grieved for the hardness of their hearts" (Mark 3:5). That is the point at which we so often fail. We become angry, not just against the sin, but against the sinner, often without pity for him in our hearts. What is right in God cannot be wrong in man insofar as he moves along the same lines and is touched by a like spirit. A mother shows more love in reproving her child than in permitting him to grow up with a disregard for the rights of others. A doctor shows more love in causing pain to a patient that will ultimately be cured than in letting him die of his malady. A judge shows more love in sentencing an offender than by letting him continue in a life of crime. There may be more love in resisting than in yielding to the evildoer. There may be more love in the sentence against than in indifference to his offense. But in both the heart of love must beat, and our resistance to evil or our judgment upon it must be directed against the sin, not the sinner.

Let us permit the life of Christ to cast light upon His words. We are not merely to obey the words, but to follow the speaker of them; we have not only a guide–book but a guide, and it is by both of these, not merely one, that we should be led. Orthopraxy, "right–doing," is our exegesis of orthodoxy, "right–thinking" (see "Non–Resistance," by W. Garrett Horder, in *The Christian World Pulpit,* 26 Feb, 1986, Vol. 49:117–19).

"The words that I speak unto you, they are spirit, and they are life," said Christ (John 6:63). Letter–of–the law Christians are as deserving of censure as were the letter–of–the–law scribes and Pharisees whom Jesus rebuked. It is possible to obey Christ's commands to the letter and totally fail to discern their original intent or the spirit that should motivate them. You can turn the other cheek in a spirit of self–righteous martyrdom that will only infuriate your assailant further. Or you can with perfect propriety rebuke him in love, and in a kindly spirit even restrain him physically from inflicting injury on you, without violating the spirit of Christ's commandment. It is retaliation that is forbidden, meeting anger with anger. By refusing to respond in kind, you demonstrate that you obey a higher law, the law of love. Take this, then, as your guiding principle in seeking to carry out the will of God with respect to resistance or non–resistance: It is the spirit that counts; love may combat, but selfishness may not.

DO YOU HAVE PEACE OF SOUL?

When we read "Blessed are the peacemakers," in Matthew 5:9, we take it for granted that we understand what Christ meant by these words. But there are many facets to this simple injunction. For instance, what direction does this peace take? Can you bring peace to others if you yourself are not at peace with God?

Your peace must first have an inward direction. Your initial concern should be to have peace in your own soul and life, for you cannot share what you do not possess. To try to do so is hypocrisy. Pity the poor souls who go to church looking for peace and have the misfortune to sit under a preacher who preaches the peace of God but has never experienced it. His words lack conviction because they are not mirrored in his life. Those who possess peace show it through their lives as well as their words. But the trouble is not altogether with the preacher. There are many sitting in the pews who know the peace of God, realize that the preacher neither has it nor preaches it, yet make no effort to share their peace with him or others who are in need of it. A peacemaker must have firm convictions about God's way of peace and be willing to do something about them. As someone has said, "It would be a great mercy if every converted person would positively refuse to listen twice to any minister who denies the inspiration of the Bible, or to give a penny to a church or missionary society that gave the right hand of fellowship to men of this type. If this were done, there would be less people in the pulpits and on the mission field whose preaching brings everything but peace to the souls of men."

What Woodrow Wilson said about preachers is worthy of the careful consideration of every one of us: "When I hear some of the things which young men say to men by way of putting the arguments to themselves for going into the ministry, I think they are talking of another profession. Their motive is to do something. You do not have to be anything in particular to be a lawyer, and I know you do not have to be anything in particular, except a kind–hearted man, perhaps, to be a physician, nor undergo any strong spiritual change in order to be a merchant. The only profession which consists in being something is the ministry of our Lord and Savior—and it does not consist of anything else. And that conception of the ministry which rubs all the marks off and mixes him in the crowd so that you cannot pick him out, is a process of eliminating the ministry itself."

Our job as preachers is to share the peace of God in our own hearts. If we do not possess it, we ought not to waste the time of others by offering them empty words, deceiving them into believing that they can find something worthwhile in our well–turned but hollow phrases.

A young preacher fresh from seminary went to the front as a chaplain. He announced to the soldiers that he would let them choose whether they wanted him to preach a sermon or tell them funny stories. A tall, blunt–speaking fellow arose and said, "If you have come three thousand miles to talk to a bunch of soldiers, some of whom are going into eternity within three days and you don't know whether to preach to them or tell them funny stories, I suspect you had just better go ahead and tell something funny." Think of it! No wonder men faint from fear, when no one is willing or able to share with them the peace of God.

The Beatitudes, including the injunction to peacemaking, are addressed primarily to Christ's disciples, who had already experienced the peace of God as a result of the forgiveness of their sins by Christ. Because this is the only way peace can come to us, it should form the basis of our preaching. Any book on peace for the troubled man of the twentieth century immediately becomes a best seller. There is a great uneasiness in the souls of men. Let's not tell them that this disturbance is the result of unjustified guilt–feelings, that it is all the product of man's sick imagination. The cause is real; the Bible calls it sin, rebellion against God. Unless man makes peace with God, he will never know peace of heart and mind.

It is said of a famous preacher that he always preached "as a dying man to dying men." Such preaching is effective. A minister visiting a penitentiary one Saturday was invited by the Christian warden to speak to the inmates the next day. That evening the minister felt that he should return to the penitentiary to learn the details regarding the service. Noting two chairs draped in black in the main assembly room, he inquired as to the reason. Said the warden, "These two chairs are draped for death. Your sermon will be the last these men will ever hear." Do you think that a funny story would have helped these men? What they needed was peace with God; they needed Christ as their Savior before they met Him as Judge. I am very conscious as I preach that there are chairs in most audiences draped for death. The peace of God in my own soul is the most precious possession I have. Like Peter and John, "Such as I have give I thee: In the name of Jesus Christ of Nazareth rise up and walk" (Acts 3:6). Sin paralyzes and deforms. Christ releases us and heals our spiritual wounds. In His healing of our souls we find peace.

We must preach what has passed through the crucible of our own experience. We shall never produce conviction in others until truth is a burning conviction in our own souls. And genuine peace can only be based upon truth. If we do not practice and preach the truth, we cannot hope either to enjoy peace or be peacemakers. Bunyan says, "I preached what I did feel, what I smartingly did feel." When David Hume, the philosopher, had listened to John Broun of Haddington, he remarked, "That's the man for me; he means what he says; he preaches as if Christ were at his elbow."

Are you at peace in your own soul? The first exercise in peacemaking is to look inward. You may be in the best of circumstances, and yet there is a secret pang that makes you ill at ease; there is a bitter thought that comes across you when first you wake in the morning; there is a something of which you do not like to speak, of which you do not like to hear, and of which, if possible, you would rather not think. That is your alienation from God. You are at war with your Creator. You need to make peace with Him through Jesus Christ, who is our peace. It hurts to recognize your sin; it is like submitting to the surgeon's knife. But look at the results—healing, forgiveness, and the peace that passeth all understanding.

For those who have already made peace with God through Jesus Christ, there is still an inward look to take. We may be going through a time of suffering, pain, sorrow, illness, and yet be in perfect peace because we are doing our God–appointed duty. It may be that our duty is only the duty of endurance, resignation, and submission. If this be clear before us, and if we resolve upon this, it is enough. "They also serve who only stand and wait." It may be that our duty involves business, public cares, or private ministrations. That, too, is enough. It shows the path before us straight and clear; it makes us indifferent to what people say or think of us; it makes us forget ourselves; it makes life worth living; it makes death welcome. "Mark the perfect man, and behold the upright," says the Psalmist, "for the end of that man is peace" (Ps. 37:37). To have said the right thing, though it cost us an effort; to have done the right thing, though it seemed hard at the time; this, you may be sure, leaves a tranquillity behind that long outlives the moment and makes us feel as if we were in a haven of rest, because the peace of conscience is indeed the peace of the Holy Spirit of Christ (see *The Anglican Pulpit Library*, London: Jack MacKenzie Ltd., n.d., Vol. 9:28).

The fact that Christ said, "Blessed are the peacemakers," shows that though it is God's desire for every one of His creatures to possess His peace, this is not the actual state of affairs No man is born with the peace of God in his heart. The natural man is not in harmony with God; he is a rebel. God has taken the initiative of bringing us back to Himself by sending His Son to die for us. But that does not automatically save an. We must appropriate God's offer. It takes two to make peace. God offers it and man accepts it. Salvation is all of grace; but man must have faith to receive it. Blessed are those who make peace with God—their own peace, yet not their own but based on the peace of God that by faith they make their very own.

Isn't it strange that when we read the words of our Master, "Blessed are the peacemakers," we think only of the role we should play in the lives of others. But we cannot play that role until we have first applied the lesson to our own hearts. Blessed is the man who has made his peace with God. No matter how long you have been at war with Him, if you will only believe on Christ, for His sake you can experience that peace for yourself This personal peacemaking is for the passionate, the fretful, the ill-tempered, the selfish, and the sinful. It begins with your own life.

The work of peace is neither superficial nor external. It is as deep as the human heart. We are accustomed to look upon the restlessness and the strife of the world as something about us, but the secret of it all is within us. It is written in the inner place of every man's life. Men are wrong with each other because they are wrong with God. Sin is the one and only disturber of the peace, and sin is the transgression of the infinite law of righteousness and love under which the soul lives. The way to peace lies through the cleansing of the inward life from all impure and selfish thoughts and purposes. It lies through the vision of God that brings with it the true vision of life. The peacemakers are to be called the sons of God because they are, indeed, the children of their Father in heaven, living out their lives in simple obedience to His will. They are not so much the sons of God because they make peace; rather they make peace because they are living in realization and acknowledgment of that sonship. The peace that a man is able to minister to the world about him is just the measure of the peace that is ever being ministered to his own heart in response to his reverence and faith and obedience and spiritual earnestness.

Entering into peace is entering into life as God means it should be lived, understanding its true significance, its priceless spiritual values, and its real issues. The peaceful—and therefore the peacemaking—life is one lived in harmony with the divine order. And the way into such harmony is a blood–stained way. The world's true peace grows out of the world's supreme tragedy. "Having made peace by the blood of his cross." The hands that are stretched forth to still the passions and the strifes of men are nail–pierced hands. The feet that go before us in the way of peace are wounded feet. The divine Peacemaker was crucified. And it is at the cross with its awful indictment of human selfishness and its tender mercy for every sinful life, that the work of peace begins. It is not possible to set forth the nature and scope of this work of peacemaking in anything but general terms. It is not a duty in life, it is a whole duty of life, to seek peace and pursue it. Every effort to be what God means us to be, and to do what God means us to do, is a real part of the high service of peace (Percy C. Ainsworth, *The Blessed Life,* London: Charles H. Kelly, 1915:147, 146).

THE FIRST QUALIFICATION OF A PEACEMAKER—UNSELFISHNESS

Christians have to get along with two classes of people in this world: those who, like themselves, are blessed because of Christ, and those who have never come to know Him as Savior. Their peacemaking activities are related to both. Sometimes it is harder to live at peace with those within the fold of Christ than with those without. Paul had his differences with Barnabas, John Mark, Peter, and James; And we, too, will experience personality clashes in our dealings with other Christians. We tend to expect perfection from those in Christ, and they expect perfection from us, but as we rub shoulders in the exercise of our daily tasks we find out that we are still human beings who are pressing toward the mark but have not fully attained. Of course, it is much easier to see the imperfections of others than our own. A Christian really needs a pair of two–way spectacles that would enable him to look as clearly inside himself as outside. There would be much more peace in the family of God if you and I started wearing such glasses.

Modern psychologists say that sometimes the faults we are most intolerant of in others are those that we secretly or unconsciously harbor in our own hearts. We have two sets of value–words in dealing with the shortcomings of others as compared to our own. We say: They are stubborn; we are firm. They are ill–tempered; we are righteously indignant. They are greedy and grasping; we are prudent and foresighted. They sometimes cut corners or are downright dishonest; we are businesslike and practical. They tell lies; we are tactful.

We all know and are amused by the overweight person who wants everyone else to go on a diet, but claims he cannot lose weight himself because overweight runs in his family. But on a larger scale this sort of self–deception is not amusing, and among Christians it makes our testimony valueless in the eyes of our brethren and the world. "Why beholdest thou the mote that is in thy brother's eye," asked our Lord, "but considerest not the beam that is in thine own eye? Or how wilt thou say to thy brother, Let me pull out the mote out of thine eye; and, behold, a beam is in thine own eye? Thou hypocrite, first cast out the beam out of thine own eye; and then shalt thou see clearly to cast out the mote out of thy brother's eye" (Matt. 7:3–5).

Yet the Christian peacemaker cannot remain indifferent to his adversaries. At the funeral of the late great Greek Evangelical leader, Dr. Constantin Metallinos, it was said that what stood out about his life was that he had no enemies. But that was only a half–truth; it described his personal attitude toward others, believers and unbelievers alike. But that could hardly have been the attitude of all others toward him, for that would have contradicted the experience and words of Christ, who said, "Ye shall be hated of all men for my name's sake" (Matt. 10:22). When Thomas a Kempis was negotiating with the proud religionists of his unevangelical day, we hear him saying, "Jesus Christ was despised of men, forsaken of His friends and lovers, and in the midst of slanders. He was willing, under His Father's will, to suffer and to be despised, and darest thou to complain of any man's usage of thee? Christ, thy Master, had enemies and backbiters, and dost thou expect to have all men to be thy friends and benefactors? Whence shall thy patience attain her promised crown if no adversity befall thee? Suffer thou with Jesus Christ, and for His sake, if thou wouldst reign with Him. Set thyself, therefore, to bear manfully the cross of thy Lord, who, out of love, was crucified for thee. Know for certain that thou must lead a daily dying life. And the more that thou diest to thyself all that the more shalt thou live unto God."

The Christian hates no man, but he is often hated for the sake of his principles. It is the duty of the peacemaker, short of sinning and compromising principle, to win his adversaries over by love.

Observe that the Greek word used in urging us to love others is the verb *agapaō,* which means to love someone, not because of what he is, but in spite of it, because of his need. God loved us, not because we were good, and pure, and lovable, but because in our sinful, lost estate we needed Him. That is the kind of love He wants us to demonstrate to others. Where would we be if God loved us only when we deserved it? We are to love our adversaries, not because they deserve it but because they need it.

Another Greek word for love used in the New Testament is *phileō,* which refers to a love based on common interests rather than the unselfish sacrifice implied in *agapē,* In our peacemaking, the Lord does not want us to love the world in the sense of *philoumen,* accommodating our principles to its sinful indulgences, but in the sense of *agapōmen,* for the sake of winning men to Jesus Christ. This love "seeketh not her own, is not easily provoked, thinketh no evil; rejoiceth not in iniquity, but rejoiceth in the truth; beareth all things, believeth all things, hopeth all things, endureth all things" (1 Cor. 13:5–7). It "suffereth long, and is kind . . . envieth not . . . vaunteth not itself, is not puffed up" (v. 5). The Christian cannot sit contentedly under the rapture of God. He cannot keep it selfishly for himself. God loved and He gave. Have you that kind of love?

A state of alienation is too painful to be borne when it can be mended. If, without loss of true honor, or practical injustice, or any other greater evil following, the offender can be won to penitence or the offended to pardon by any humbling on our part or by personal loss and pain, the pure heart will be pressed out of itself to win its brother, as God in Christ has won us. The peacemaker then loves with a divine love that is not won over to sin but that woos the sinner to Calvary.

In our mission of peacemaking, as we seek to demonstrate love to those who rub shoulders with us in life, whether they be believers or unbelievers, we must recognize and correct those tendencies in ourselves that would break the peace rather than promote it. The first direction of our peacemaking must be inward.

There must be no stinging conscience, no unsatisfied desire, no inner schism between inclination and duty, reason and will, passion and judgment. There must be the quiet of a harmonized nature which has one object, one aim, one love, without contradictions running through the inmost self. There is only one way to get that peace—cleaving to Jesus Christ and making Him our Lord, our righteousness, our aim, our all. Your conscience will sting, and that destroys peace; or, if it does not sting, it will be torpid, and that destroys peace, for death is not peace. Unless we take Christ for our love, for the light of our minds, for the Sovereign Arbiter and Lord of our will, for the home of our desires, for the aim of our efforts, we shall never know what it is to reproduce His gentleness, sympathy, compassion, insight into men's sorrows, patience with men's offenses, and all which makes, in our relations to one another, the harmony and the happiness of humanity.

The primary disturber of the peace in our own lives and the lives of others is our lusts and passions, our appetites and desires. If we are greedy and are not satisfied with what God has been pleased to give us, and we place our passions first, we will disturb the peace of contentment within ourselves and the peace of others.

We may thus destroy the peace of our own homes, of wife, of husband, of children. The craving for self–satisfaction, the desire to have everybody contribute to our physical or spiritual wants, is the greatest peacebreaker imaginable. Peacemaking love must attend a funeral—the funeral of its own self—before Christ can work in and through us and His glory be reflected in us and by us.

A selfish man can neither be peaceful nor a peace maker. He cares intensely and continually for his own wants, however minute, and nothing for the greater distress of his brother, however pressing. He seeks his own advantage; and if the way to it should lead through chaos, amid bloodshed, a universal disquiet, it matters not to him. His object is to gratify himself, and he is prepared to sacrifice others in the process. Abbe Grou says, "Self–love makes us touchy, ready to take offense, ill–tempered, suspicious, severe, exacting, easily offended; it keeps alive in our hearts a certain malignity, a secret joy at the mortifications which befall our neighbor; it nourishes our readiness to criticize, our dislike at certain persons, our ill–feeling, our bitterness, and a thousand other things prejudicial to charity."

Let it be stated, then, that the first qualification of a peacemaker is unselfishness, for only in the spirit of Christ can he bring Christ's peace to others.

THE CHARACTERISTICS OF THE PEACEMAKER

We have seen that a selfish man can never be peaceful or a peacemaker. The first beatitude established the basis of all our peacemaking—poverty of spirit or humility. Without humility no one can be a peacemaker: and no selfish person can be humble. The would–be peacemaker cannot mount to the seventh rung of the ladder of Christian blessedness without having taken the first step of humility, without having fulfilled the first condition of blessedness—humbling himself before God. There can be no skipping of rungs on this ladder, though many Christians have tried and are trying to do just that. That is why so many undertaking the professional task of peacemaking turn out to be peacebreakers. As Alexander Whyte says, "Every man who is to be the minister of a parish should make his own heart and his own life his first parish. His own vineyard should be his first knowledge and his first care. And then out of that and after that he will be able to speak to his people, and to correct, and counsel, and take care of them. In Thomas Boston's *Memoirs* we continually come on entries like this: 'Preached on Psalm 42:5, and mostly on my own account.' And, again, we read in the same invaluable book for parish ministers, that its author did not wonder to hear that good had been done by last Sabbath's sermon, because he had preached it to himself and had got good to himself out of it before he took it to the pulpit."

If you are not humble, you cannot fulfill the rest of Christ's commandments in the Beatitudes. When we know ourselves as we are, and see ourselves in the light of God, we learn to lie low in the dust, to think others better than ourselves, and to wonder that so great grace has been manifested by God to us so unworthy. When one thus feels humbled in the sight of God, he will show himself most tender, most unselfish, in the sight of and in his relationships to man. He feels that his place is larger than he deserves, his fame greater than he merits, his blessings far richer than he ever dreamed of; and he will be so overwhelmed by the sight of the good things that he has and his sense of unworthiness, that he will have no time to pick quarrels with a brother. He rejoices at the prosperity of every one who he thinks is better than himself and of whom he can only entertain the most charitable and kindly apprehensions.

The second trio of Beatitudes following the fourth beatitude of hungering and thirsting after righteousness has to do with our relations to others. Before God we have to be humble, mournful, meek, and before men we have to be merciful, pure, and peacemaking. As Alexander Maclaren says: "The climax of Christian character, according to Jesus Christ Himself, is found in our relations to men, and not in our relation to God. Worship of heart and spirit, devout emotions of the sacredest, sweetest, most hallowed and hallowing sort, are absolutely indispensable. But equally, if not more, important is it for us to remember that the purest communion with God, and the selectest emotional experiences of the Christian life, are meant to be the bases of active service: and that, if it does not follow these, there is good reason for supposing that these are spurious, and worth very little. The service of man is the outcome of the love of God. He who begins with poverty of spirit is perfected when, forgetting himself, and coming down from the mountain–top, where the Shekinah cloud of the glory and the audible voice are, he plunges into the struggles of the multitude below, and frees the devil–ridden boy from the demon that possessed him. Begin by all means with poverty of spirit, or you will never get to this—'Blessed are the peace-makers.' But see to it that poverty of spirit leads to the meekness, the mercifulness, the peace–bringing influence which Christ has pronounced blessed" (*The Beatitudes and Other Sermons,* London: Hodden and Stroughton, 1903: 66, 67).

"That man knows little of himself," says Alexander Whyte, "who does not despise himself for his secret self–seeking even in the service of God. For how the love of praise will seduce and corrupt this man, and the love of gain that man! How easy it is to flatter and adulate this man out of all his former opinions and his deepest principles, and how an expected advantage will make that other man forget now an old alliance and now a deep antipathy! How often the side we take even in the most momentous matters is decided by the most unworthy motives and the most contemptible considerations!"

From selfishness springs covetousness. The covetous person cannot be a peacemaker, because he thirsts to fill his coffers with the riches of the world. Gold is his God. What fills our calendars with crime? What makes our courts of law echo with ceaseless lawsuits? The love of money. Probably the love of money is the greatest peacebreaker upon earth. There is a pathetic passage in Dickens' *Christmas Carol* in which Scrooge, escorted by the "Ghost of Christmas Past," sees himself as a much younger man. "His face had not the harsh and rigid lines of later years; but it had begun to wear the signs of care and avarice. He was not alone, but sat by the side of a fair young girl in a mourning–dress, in whose eyes there were tears, which sparkled in the light that shone out of the 'Ghost of Christmas Past.'

" 'It matters little,' she said softly. 'To you very little. Another idol has displaced me; and if it can cheer and comfort you in time to come, as I would have tried to do, I have not just cause to grieve.'

" 'What idol has displaced you?' he rejoined.

" 'A golden one.' "

Although Scrooge tried to protest that his love for his betrothed was as strong as ever, his words were lame and half-hearted. She gave him back his engagement ring. So Scrooge shut love of humankind out of his life and gave himself wholly over to love of gold.

If you wish to be a peacemaker, begin by being loving and generous. We are each different from the other. Some of us are naturally generous and some of us are misers. But whatever our natural dispositions, we must remember that when we become Christians we are supernaturally transformed into new beings in Christ Jesus. By your generosity you manifest your degree of blessedness and peacemaking.

In your selfishness you may not be thirsty for gold but for glory. This, too, can shatter the peace of your own soul and of others. What causes wars? Ambition for glory. Hitler was driven by it to the slaughter of millions. Communism is ambitious and therefore reckless. Analyze the wars within the portals of our churches. The cause will be found in the inordinate selfish ambitions of some individuals, the pastor not excluded. Let one man, one woman acquire the thirst for glory in a congregation and peace disappears.

The Apostle John, in writing to Gaius, in his Third Epistle, speaks of such a one: "I wrote unto the church," he says, "but Diotrephes, who loveth to have the preeminence among them, receiveth us not. Wherefore, if I come, I will remember his deeds which he doeth, prating against us with malicious words: and not content therewith, neither doth he himself receive the brethren, and forbiddeth them that would, and casteth them out of the church" (vv. 9, 10). How many like Diotrephes disrupt the peace of the Church today! Let them take heed to the word of the Lord in Jeremiah 45:5, "Seekest thou great things for thyself? seek them not."

The thirst for power, for aggrandizement and renown, has been one of the greatest peacebreakers in the history of mankind, internationally, nationally, and within our communities, churches, and families. And sometimes peacebreaking ambition is very viciously and deceitfully disguised as service to mankind. The ambitious man wants to become as powerful as possible so he can dictate peace. But the peace of the ambitious is usually the peace of tyranny; and war, open war for individual freedom, is far better than the uninvited peace imposed by an ambitious tyrant.

LIVING AT PEACE WITH OTHERS

When we have made peace with God in our own souls through receiving Christ as our Savior and yielding to Him as Lord, we are ready to direct our peacemaking outward, toward others. As we apply this beatitude inwardly, it is evangelism for our own hearts, and as we direct it outwardly it is a missionary message for others. We are to proclaim to the world that Christ has made peace through the blood of His cross, and we are to be willing to share this peace at all costs.

A business girl, who was having a very hard time among her friends and suffering much persecution for her Christian testimony, came to an evangelist who was holding a series of special Sunday evening services in a large public auditorium and told him she was afraid she must give it all up. He said to her, "Tell me, where do we put the lights?" She looked puzzled at his question, so he answered it for her: "We put the lights in a dark place." In a moment she saw his meaning and realized that God had put her in difficult surroundings that she might shine for Jesus in the midst of darkness. She went back determined to be more courageous than ever in her witness for Christ. A few weeks later, after the evening service, she came to him with a group of other girls, all radiant with joy. "Oh," she said, "the thirteenth from our office has decided for Christ tonight!"

It would certainly be a watering down of Christ's message to conceive of this beatitude in its outward expression as merely an endeavor on our part to live agreeably with others. A person who possesses the peace of God is also possessed of divine principles. And where there is principle there must be division when these principles are transgressed. This is what the Lord intimated when He said, "I am come to send fire on the earth; and what will I, if it be already kindled? But I have a baptism to be baptized with; and how am I straitened till it be accomplished! Suppose ye that I am come to give peace on earth? I tell you, Nay; but rather division: For from henceforth there shall be five in one house divided, three against two, and two against three. The father shall be divided against the son, and the son against the father; the mother against the daughter, and the daughter against the mother; the mother–in–law against her daughter-in-law, and the daughter–in–law against her mother in law" (Luke 12:49–53).

Compromise with sin and the sinner can never be conceived of as New Testament peacemaking. Our peacemaking efforts must go far deeper than that, not simply seeking to change the circumstances of people's lives but their very hearts, through leading them to Christ, so that they can see God and cooperate with His will in the circumstances of their lives. Then, instead of grumbling, we shall have praise and instead of rebellion, peace. The circumstances remain the same, but the person is changed. Blessed are the peacemakers and also those to whom they bring peace. They cannot bring peace to others by sharing their material possessions or providing for their bodily needs—although Christ's peacemakers will want to relieve human need and suffering—but by proclaiming the gospel of reconciliation. Remember Christ's eternal words, "A man's life consisteth not in the abundance of the things which he possesseth" (Luke 12:15). "Godliness with contentment is great gain" (1 Tim. 6:6).

This is how it worked with Aquilla. He was lame from birth, and as he sat by his window propped up in a chair and watched the other boys playing in the street, he asked, "Why has God made me thus? Why have I not feet and legs to run and jump as other boys? O God!" he exclaimed, "I am angry with you! Away with God! Away with religion!" He was full of sharpness, and sourness, and complaint. His disposition was bitter, and this bitter disposition shed bitterness on all the world around. But a friend came in one day who loaned him a Christian book. Aquilla read this book, and it opened new thoughts to him. Step by step he was led along until he saw himself as a sinner and his faith laid hold on Christ. The burden of sin was removed; his heart was renewed; the love of God was shed abroad in his heart by the Holy Ghost. Now, as he saw the people passing his window while he was confined to his chair, he said, "It is all right. God has done it. My Father has done it. I love Him. He loves me. He can but do all things for my good." Where there had been war there was peace, with a friend and a book as the peacemakers.

This beatitude not only means that we should bring the peace of God to those who know Him not; it has a bearing on our day–to–day relations with them. Short of compromising with sin, we who are blessed in Christ are admonished, "as much as lieth in you, live peaceably with all men" (Rom. 12:18). This means that the Christian should strive for the highest possible degree of peaceful coexistence consistent with not sacrificing principle or allowing evil to overrun good. There is a point at which the Christian must break with the world; he is to live in the world but not become worldly. Men and women cannot become one outside of Christ; but we must relate to them in such a way that they will desire the peace that we manifest. The Christian should seek, "as much as lieth in him," to be attractive and not repulsive to those who are not Christians. The way we live should cause others to be disturbed and at the same time drawn to us.

This injunction to live peaceably with all men also applies to the household of faith. Christians are to live at peace with one another. Though members of the same family of God, and redeemed by the same blood of the cross, we are all different in appearance, in the way we think, speak, and act. The Christian who wants everyone else to be like him is a peacebreaker. In his spiritual pride he wants to set himself up as the model Christian. If the other person does not think as he does, he is not spiritual. Beware, you who set yourselves up as a standard of spirituality to which you feel others should conform. The greatest peacebreaker in Christendom is he who appoints himself judge over others. No one is comfortable in his presence. On any committee he wants to run the whole show or he will not cooperate. He is heady, intolerant, harsh, dogmatic, censorious. Young Christians are discouraged by his constant faultfinding. Older Christians are repelled by his demand that they concur in his unkind judgments. He is an irritant wherever he goes. Inward peace and outward peacemaking are foreign to his nature. How different was the spirit of Alexander Pope, who wrote:

> Let not this weak, unknowing hand
> Presume Thy bolts to throw,
> And deal damnation round the land
> On each I judge Thy foe.
>
> If I am right, Thy grace impart
> Still in the right to stay:
> If I am wrong, oh teach my heart
> To find a better way.
>
> Save me alike from foolish pride
> Or impious discontent,
> At aught Thy wisdom has denied,
> Or aught Thy goodness lent.
>
> Teach me to feel another's woe,
> To hide the fault I see;
> That mercy I to others show,
> That mercy show to me.

Let us recognize the diversity in our physical and spiritual makeups, even as in nature there is diversity with overall harmony. The world would be a dull place, indeed, very different from what God intended it to be, if all of us thought, spoke, and acted alike. The world of nature derives its beauty and its grace from the ups and downs, the rents and fissures, the straits and seas which cut it asunder and give it all its various shapes and forms. So it is with the world of man. We must allow men to differ. We cannot force everyone into the same mold of character, pursuits, tastes, and opinions. But here, as in the natural world, we can and should prevent any difference, except the difference of sin, from becoming a separation.

The word "pontiff," used to designate the highest religious order of the Roman Catholic Church, namely the Pope, has an interesting history. This was the name which, in the old pagan religion of ancient Rome, was given to the chief priests. The pontiffs were those who were invested with pontifical power. The name as it was first applied meant "the makers of bridges." Why it was so used in the first instance we hardly know. Those old Roman pontiffs were, perhaps, specially employed in consecrating those mighty instruments of earthly peace and civilization, the great roads and bridges by which the old Romans tamed and subdued the world. But in a moral and spiritual sense we ought all to be makers of bridges. Pontiff or no pontiff, minister or no minister, every Christian who walks in his Master's steps ought to make it his special business to throw bridges across those moral rents and fissures which divide us one from the other. Across these various gulfs and chasms let every one lend a helping hand to build such bridges as best we can. There cannot be a more truly pontifical work.

PRACTICAL POINTS ON PEACEMAKING

"Though I speak with the tongues of men and of angels," said Paul, "and have not love, I am become as sounding brass, or a tinkling cymbal. And though I . . . understand all mysteries . . . and have not love, I am nothing" (1 Cor. 13:1, 2). Likewise, if you and I understand all that is involved in Christian peacemaking, and do not apply it, it is useless knowledge. Therefore I would like to offer a few practical suggestions for those who want to take this task of peacemaking seriously.

Cultivate a forgiving spirit. Be "easily entreated," as Scripture puts it. Anger is not sinful when it is for the right cause and at the right time; but when it degenerates, or rather kindles, into revenge, then it becomes one of the most hateful occupants of the human heart. It is insulted where insult may not have been designed; if it burns in an individual soul it challenges to a conflict of words or even a physical struggle; if in a nation, it instantly provokes or challenges to war. Revenge, whether in individuals or nations, becomes one of the great peacebreakers.

Cultivate a spirit of contentment. Where envy reigns, there is a man prepared to quarrel, and of all passions it is the most contemptible. Envy is not a desire that I should be blessed or benefited, but that my brother should be dragged down from his eminence, even if I should remain on the same dead level to which I would reduce him. When this passion gets full possession of the human heart, it is a corroding pain within and its calamitous consequences without are too frequently seen; they are written in some of the darkest pages of history.

Be slow to resent slights or injuries. When men speak ill of you, unless it be something that demands instant and public reply, let it alone. "Every time," says J. R. Miller, "we keep silent under insult, and loving and sweet under provocation, we have made it easier for all about us to do the same." Especially exercise the grace of silence or the power of gentleness in your own home. Your wife or husband or child or mother says something to you that kindles resentment. Don't ask for an explanation and apology. Find a way to show that Christ dwells in your heart, not by descending to the level of the offender, but by identifying with Christ in attitude and word, so that the peacebreaker cannot but look up to you as an example of forbearance, patience, and longsuffering. Words spoken in anger and resentment are like rubber balls thrown against a wall. The harder the surface you bounce them against the harder they fly back at you. Love seeks to find justification for many actions that grieve it. If you really love your wife or husband or pastor or friend, you'll try to justify the motivation although you will condemn the act. But let the condemnation remain unspoken, and at the same time let a prayer ascend to God for the offender's correction. You don't really want to destroy the person you love, but win him over.

Be slow to listen to rumors, and above all those about a brother, when these reach you prophesying evil, when others look only at the bad side of his conduct, reject it at once, until incontrovertibly demonstrated to be true. Suspect the person who always whispers in your ear something he does not want anyone else to hear. In reality it is the opposite that he desires. In every community there are those who go about retelling gossip, the tendency of which is to separate friends. Every Christian should be a discourager of talebearing. Too many people encourage it. They are glad to hear something unpleasant about another and are quick to pass it on. Such eagerness is not commendable and does not have upon it the blessing of peacemaking.

> If you are tempted to reveal
> A tale someone to you has told
> About another, make it pass,
> Before you speak, three gates of gold.
>
> Three narrow gates: First, "Is it true?"
> Then, "Is it needful?" In your mind
> Give truthful answer. And the next
> Is last and narrowest—"Is it kind?"
>
> And if to reach your lips at last
> It passes through these gateways three,
> Then you may tell the tale, nor fear
> What the result of speech may be.
>
> —Author Unknown

Refrain from sowing doubt and suspicion of others in people's minds. That is not the office of a peacemaker. One often learns, in close fellowship with others, that two neighbors or friends are in danger of becoming enemies. Now is the opportunity for the peacemaker's ministry. Instead of aggravating the little beginning of bitterness, as he may do by a word of encouragement, he should set about to try to heal the breach and restore confidence. Usually it is not hard to do this. Many quarrels begin in a slight misunderstanding, and a few words spoken by a true–hearted peacemaker will show, first to one and then to the other, that there is really no cause for ill–feeling, that the doubt of loyalty is unjust, and that a separation or an estrangement is not only unnecessary but would be positively sinful.

When over the fair fame of friend or foe
    The shadow of disgrace shall fall; instead
Of words of blame, or proof of thus and so,
    Let something good be said.

Forget not that no fellow–being yet
    May fall so low but love may lift his head;
Even the cheek of shame with tears is wet
    If something good be said.

And so I charge ye, by the thorny crown
    And by the cross on which the Saviour bled,
And by your own soul's hope of fair renown,
    Let something good be said.

—James Whitcomb Riley

A true peacemaker, going about thus, trying to draw people ever closer together and to heal all threatened contentions and quarrels, is doing a divine work of love in the world. The great majority of strifes among men are needless. They are caused by the meddlesomeness of outside parties. Or they come from hasty words or acts unconfessed and unrepented of. The peacemaker's word, spoken at the right moment, would prevent all this (see J. R. Miller, *The Garden of the Heart,* London: Hodder and Stroughton, 1903:250–259).

Those who have been estranged for one reason or another stand very little chance of ever establishing peace between themselves because they tend to avoid each other. The Christian peacemaker can at least try to bring about a meeting between them. Use your home as a house of peace. Within its portals let there reign the peace of God, so that when others come in they cannot but be awed by it. Those at war with their relatives and fellow men will see that peace is not an impossibility and that the absence of it from their particular environment may be their own fault.

All true peacemakers think things through. It does not take brains to destroy, but it does take thought to build. A house-wrecker needs no university training, but an architect does. Think before you speak, and your speech is more likely to promote peace. Forbear in speech when a word is ready to escape from your lips that would kindle a conflagration. Stop to think before you lift your hand to strike. Count the reaction and the end result. Forbear in hand, when your action might be violent and destructive. Think your thoughts over when they might prompt to revenge. Very high in the records of peacemaking stand the names of those who in every age have brought to the problems of life the acumen of a finely–tempered reason, yoked with the simple and safe instincts of a clean heart. These have ever given to the world true views of God and life, and we are called to share not merely in the gains of their toil but in the toil itself. There is a scholarship of sanctity, a wisdom of the heart, within reach of us all; and so far as we learn to think truly about our Father in heaven and the life He would have us live on the earth, we may find some place in the ministry of light that leads to the way of peace (see Percy C. Ainsworth, *The Blessed Life,* London: Charles H. Kelly, 1915:152).

It is thought, sanctified thought, that will show us when to resist and when not to resist, when and how to speak and strike. When Christ said, "Give to him that asketh thee," was He advocating indiscriminate charity? We should not allow ourselves to be deceived by impostors, but neither should we harden our hearts and do nothing. In my life, I prefer to be deceived than to deprive a worthy individual of help. We must exercise judgment, though, both in peacemaking and in charity. "The easy wrong things to do," says A. D. Lindsay, "are to give without thought, and not to give, again without thought. We owe people our clear thought as well as our kind heart. We ought to give to him that asketh us, but not always what he asks; and it often takes a great deal more pain and trouble and thought to give people what they need than to give them what they wish. To take these verses as simple rules, requiring of us lots of will to do, but no thought to interpret, is really moral laziness, and can clearly do much harm" (*The Moral Teaching of Jesus,* London: Hodder and Stroughton, 1938:107–108).

CHILDREN OF GOD

Each of the Beatitudes of Christ contains a condition to be fulfilled in order to attain the blessedness it promises, as well as a reward for its fulfillment. In the seventh beatitude the condition is peacemaking and the reward is to "be called the children of God." This may not sound like much, but there are great spiritual riches involved in it. The greatest award that can come to my man is to receive recognition as a child of God. Paul tells us, "And if children, then heirs; heirs of God, and joint–heirs with Jesus Christ" (Rom. 8:17). Such men are the most blessed, the richest, the most joyous creatures of earth. They dwell in this world, but they are really citizens of heaven.

Who gives this recognition to the peacemaker? It is God Himself. To consider yourself a child of God proves nothing. People's estimates of themselves are notoriously untrustworthy, as witness the mental patients who harbor delusions of grandeur about themselves and their friends. A man may call himself the closest friend of the President of the United States; but that is really up to the president to say. Many people who think they are the children of God, God never recognizes as such.

We see, then, that God does not recognize as His children all whom He has created. Unregenerate men have broken their filial relationship to God. That is why, after the fall of man, you find man possessing little consciousness of God as Father. He calls Him Jehovah. God, on the other hand, has never considered Himself anything but a Father to all His creation. To estranged children, however, the feelings of God have little value. The lower orders of creatures are shut out from all participation in the gifts that belong to the higher forms of life, simply because they are so made and organized that those gifts cannot find entrance into their nature. Always and necessarily the capacity for reception must precede and determine the bestowment of blessings. Thus we have the peculiar situation that God is always the Father but not all men are His children. This is the reason we hardly ever find it stated in Scripture that, when man believes and accepts Christ as Savior and Lord and is thus born–again, God becomes his Father. Instead, the Scripture states that man becomes His child.

Thus, in this seventh beatitude, the reward of peacemaking is not stated as God becoming the Father of the peacemakers, but as the peacemakers being known as the children of God. The change is on man's part and not on God's, for God is ever unchangeable in His character. What He bestows here is divine recognition of the change in man. When you and I become His children through faith in His Son, He recognizes us as such. He treats us like sons. He makes us heirs of all that He is and all that He possesses.

This recognition by God is progressive. It comes to us first when we are born–again. "But as many as received him, to them gave he power to become the sons of God, even to them that believe on his name" (John 1:12). That capacity to believe is a distinct characteristic of men and it is distinctly a gift of God. Actually it is the only possible sensibility upon which the Spirit of God can work to woo us back to His fatherhood. The prodigal son knew instinctively that he would be accepted by the father when he returned home repentant. The moment you, as a sinner, do the same, God will accept you with great joy. He will say, "You are my child now, since you have come back to Me through My Son, the Lord Jesus Christ, whom I sent to reconcile you to Me."

After this initial recognition by God, there is a growing consciousness of our sonship to God and His kinship to us. We find a parallel here with the physical relationship between a child and his parents. As the child grows, he realizes more and more that he belongs to his parents. And the more he realizes the love, power, and provision of his parents, the greater his attachment to them and the boldness of his expectations of them. This is why, in the maturity of our Christian life, we are admonished to approach the throne of God's grace boldly. Also, with growth comes a progressive increase in likeness. When does a child look more like his parents, at birth or in later life? Family resemblance develops with growth.

When this beatitude states, "Blessed are the peacemakers: for they shall be called the children of God," it makes plain that the family likeness will be recognizable. Note that it does not say that peacemakers shall *be* God's children; rather it says that they shall be *called by* that name. If a man is not a child of God to begin with, he cannot be a peacemaker, for how can he bring the peace of God to others if he does not possess it himself? No one can be a peacemaker who is not "blessed"—that is, indwelt by God—to start with. If he is not blessed, he cannot be a peacemaker; and if he is a peacemaker, he is already a child of God.

Here we have sonship verified through likeness, as when children grown to age reproduce the parental characteristics and tread in the father's footsteps. If God's children are not only to be, but to be declared, His sons, it is not enough to be secret disciples, hiding their vision of Him. Forth into the evil, hostile world they must go, as did the proper Son of His love. Into the Son's task they too must enter. Possessing purity of heart may make us like God inwardly, but actively engaging in a ministry of peacemaking and reconciliation of mankind to God will be following in our Lord's footsteps.

It is your likeness to Christ when you are a peacemaker that is readily recognized, not only by God Himself, but by all who observe you. Do those who watch us and listen to us find it easy to tell who our Father is, whose likeness we bear? When you make the very work that Christ came to do—bringing peace to sinful men and women—the passion of your life, how can others refrain from calling you a child of God? From the time of His prophesied incarnation, Christ was called the Prince of Peace. Not until you become the bearer of His peace to others can you have this unique distinction, not of becoming a child of God, but of being called a child of God. Not until you come to the seventh beatitude do you have this reward. You can exemplify all the graces of the preceding Beatitudes: you can be poor in spirit (humble), mournful, meek, hungering and thirsting after righteousness, merciful, pure in heart. But not until you assume this holiest and highest task of peacemaking are you most discernible as a child of God. You have been His child ever since you received Christ into your heart by faith, but now, when there is an identity of vocation between you and Christ, you are the most Christlike.

It is said of Fenelon that he had such communion with God his very face shone. Lord Peterborough, a skeptic, was obliged to spend the night with him at an inn. In the morning he rushed away, saying, "If I stay another night with that man I shall be a Christian in spite of myself."

Fenelon's manners were full of grace, his voice full of love, and his face full of glory. The invitation, "Come to Jesus," was in every act. He was a "spiritual magnet." That is what we all can be, by just yielding up all to Christ, and letting Him live again in us. Under no other condition can this transforming power fulfill its peacemaking mission to our own souls or enable us to bring peace to the souls of others.

This recognition of our Godlikeness is by no means general. It is primarily a recognition by God Himself in this life and more especially in the day when we shall appear before Him in heaven. Every time you engage in bringing the peace of God to some heart and life, you may have the witness of this in your own soul. "You are My child," He says to you. "You are like Me; your work is the same as Mine." There can be nothing more satisfying in life. It is more to be desired than anything else. In fact, if we have that, we have everything.

A little lad stopped at a door and heard a young man singing, "My Father is rich in houses and lands." Disgusted that anyone should brag about his father's wealth, the child was about to turn away when the rest of the song caught his ear. "He holdeth the wealth of the world in His hands! Of rubies and diamonds, of silver and gold, His coffers are full; He has riches untold."

"Boy, I wish his father was mine!" said the boy.

"I'm the child of a King, the child of a King," the song went on.

"Now how can that be?" wondered the child. "We have no king, and I know good and well his father isn't the president."

"With Jesus, my Savior, I'm the child of a King," concluded the singer.

Then the lad knew he was singing of God. Yes, our Father is rich, and all His riches are ours. Therefore, no matter what our suffering or privations for His sake now, we can still sing:

> A tent or a cottage, why should I care?
> They're building a palace for me over there!
> Tho' exiled from home, yet still I may sing,
> "All glory to God, I'm the child of a King."
>
> —Harriet E. Buell

John perceived the greatness of this privilege when he wrote, "Behold, what manner of love the Father hath bestowed upon us, that we should be called the sons of God" (1 John 3:1).

THE CHRISTIAN'S HIGHEST CALLING

The peacemaker has the supreme joy in this life of hearing God's whisper in his heart, "You are my child, in whom I am well pleased." Others in the family of God will also recognize him as one of themselves, for spiritual things are spiritually discerned. But to the world, peacemakers may look like fools, passing up the opportunity to acquire riches, fame, and secular recognition for the sake of serving God. This should not surprise us. Paul has warned us that it would be so. "But the natural man receiveth not the things of the Spirit of God: for they are foolishness unto him: neither can he know them, because they are spiritually discerned" (1 Cor. 2:14). And some not only fail to recognize the Godlikeness of our peacemaking efforts, not only call us fools, but actively persecute us, as we see in the next beatitude (Matt. 5:10). Our peacemaking interferes with their warring and the profits derived from it. Yet this can in no way take away from the joy of our reward.

Though God will call us His children, and other Christians will recognize us as such, His enemies will fight against us. Our peacemaking will awaken hostility. This is the sword aroused by peace. They will hate us as they hated our Master, who came not only to bring peace but a sword. They will take up stones to cast at us just as they did against Him. But this will serve only to manifest afresh our Godlikeness. It is really an indirect recognition of our likeness to Christ. As we actively engage in peacemaking, there will be crosses for us even as there was a cross for Him. That will be the zenith, the apex of our peacemaking. That is when our spirit is closest to His, and safest in His keeping. The nails driven by the crucifiers only drive us closer to the heart of God, bringing more clearly to us His whisper, "You are my child; that is why you are here, suffering as I suffered."

There is no definite article before "God" in the expression, "children of God," in this beatitude. It does not read, "They shall be called the children of *the* God." In English, of course, you could not use such a construction, but in Greek it would have been grammatically possible to say *huioi tou theou,* "children of *the* God." Instead it says *huioi theou,* "children of God." Why in the immediately preceding beatitude does the Greek construction read, "Blessed are the pure in heart: for they shall see *the* God," and here say, "Blessed are the peacemakers: for they shall be called children of God," omitting the definite article? When the definite article is omitted in such cases, it is God in His totality, in His general makeup and infinity, that is meant (see *Grammar of the Greek Language,* by William Edward Jelf, John Henry and James Parker, 1859, Vol. 2:124. Also see the author's booklet, *Can Man See God?*

We are called children of God as we engage in peacemaking. But the word "God" does not merely refer to one of the three personalities of the Godhead but to all three together. It refers not only to the visible manifestations of deity but to deity itself, to God in His unity, in His eternity, and in His infinity. We are the visible peacemaker, the children of the invisible God, the only true Peacemaker, the eternal and infinite Prince of Peace. What an expressive thought this is! In the work of salvation, of bringing peace to the heart of man, all three persons of the Triune God take part. God the Father welcomes the repentant sinner, God the Son paid the penalty of his sin, and God the Holy Spirit woos the sinner, convicts him of his sin, and brings him to a realization of his need of a Savior.

Similarly we, in our task of peacemaking, need the supernatural activity of God the Father, God the Son, and God the Holy Spirit. How confident and fearless the assurance of such eternal and infinite power operating in our behalf makes us as we declare and apply the peace of God. No wonder it passes all human understanding. No human agency, psychological, philosophical, or theological, can bring God's peace to man's soul. It requires the converging of all the faculties of the eternal Godhead—Father, Son, and Holy Spirit. What a privilege is ours even to be given the opportunity of having the least share in this divine peacemaking. And because of the greatness of our small part we are called the children of the infinite and eternal God.

The Greek word used for children in this verse is *huioi* rather than *tekna*. Lexicographer Hermann Cremer tells us that frequently *teknon* is distinguished from *huios* in that *teknon* expresses the origin, *huios* the fellowship of life (*Biblico–Theological Lexicon of New Testament Greek,* London: T & T Clark, 1895:554). *Huios,* the word used in this beatitude, stresses the dignity and character of the relationship. *Tekna,* as used in John 1:12, stresses the initial establishment of a relationship to God as a Father, a matter of belonging to Him. The peacemaker is recognized as a Christian of growth and maturity, although in his relationship to God he is still characterized as a child. The Christian peacemaker enjoys the highest degree of fellowship with God. He can feel God's passionate throb for the sinner and share in it. He is a child with mature understanding of the innermost feelings and desires of God as they pertain to His creatures. He understands the dignity and character of his relationship to God and honors it. He is a child who has become a worker together with God, a partner in the salvation of disturbed and guilty sinners.

The definite article is also omitted before the word *huioi,* "children." The English translation is inaccurate when it says, "Blessed are the peacemakers: for they shall be called *the* children of God." In the Greek text it is simply "children of God." If the definite article had been used, emphasis would have been placed on the origin and the belonging instead of on the fellowship of life. It would carry the connotation that only the peacemakers are the children of God, while we know that peacemaking is a high calling and development of those who are already children of the new birth. It is not merely because we are peacemakers that we are called children of God. Many born–again Christians are not peacemakers. In fact, very few in the redeemed and regenerated family of God are peacemakers. Of those who are, it was not their peacemaking that made them God's children initially; they were already that or they wouldn't have become peacemakers at all. These are children of God par excellence, accorded that recognition here and now, who will be more fully rewarded when the final accounting of our being and doing is held in heaven. The peacemakers are not the only children of God, nor are all the children of God peacemakers. Peace making is a high distinction of fellowship and a fuller realization of our relationship with God as Father. When any of us are so distinguished of God, He calls us in a special way His children. This is most satisfying and rewarding.

The demonstrative pronoun *autoi* is used in this seventh beatitude, as in the previous one, further to emphasize this distinction of the peacemakers. Blessed are the peacemakers; for they themselves (*autoi*) shall be called children of God. It is they above all, so to speak. To them especially is afforded this great honor to be called children: not only partakers of God's nature but also sharers of His concern for sinners, and naturally sharers also of His sufferings. With all this in mind, we find Romans 8:17 taking on added meaning: "And if children, then heirs; heirs of God, and joint–heirs with Christ, if so be that we suffer with him, that we may be also glorified together." The peacemaking, of which the seventh beatitude speaks, elevates the child of God to the position of sharing not only in the accomplished work of Christ, but also in the process and method by which that accomplishment was achieved. The peacemaker takes advantage of the offer of salvation as all who wish to become Christians must; but he goes on to accept the responsibility of the suffering that is involved in the sharing of that blood–bought peace.

Suffering together in fellowship holy,
    Sharing His sorrows, His treatment, His shame;
Though man despise me because I am lowly,
    Mine is an honor which no one can name.

I am an heir to all treasures immortal,
    Heir to the Father, joint heir with the Son;
And just beyond, where I stand on the portal,
    I shall reign with Him, because we are one.

Lord, grant that now I may faithfully serve Thee,
    Since I am one with Thee, help me, I pray;
That by my life, and my words, I may praise Thee,
    And may exalt Thee, dear Savior, each day.

—Author Unknown